I0006750

The Art of Persuasion

Marketing ANYTHING in the Digital Age

by

Nathan Venture. D

To You,

Thank you!

Table of Contents

Introduction:
Embracing the Digital Revolution in Marketing

In an age where our lives interlace with digital threads, marketing stands at the forefront of evolution. Gone are the days when billboards and print ads reigned supreme; in their place, pixels and digital impressions now drive consumer decisions. At the heart of the transformation lies a deeply rooted strategy: persuasion. This introduction is your step towards mastering the influential force of digital marketing in a world that's consistently online.

The digital marketing landscape isn't just changing; it's evolving at breakneck speed. Professionals, entrepreneurs, and business owners now find themselves in a race to keep pace with technology, trends, and tactics that can make or break their online presence. The mastery of digital channels offers a bevy of tools to sculpt a brand's image, sculpting awareness, nurturing interest, and driving conversions through meticulously crafted messaging.

Imagine the digital realm as an ocean, vast and filled with opportunities and challenges alike. The businesses that learn to ride the waves of this ocean are the ones that not only survive but thrive. It's not enough to simply exist online; brands must resonate, engage, and sway in harmony with the ebb and flow of digital consumer behavior.

This revolution calls for a new set of navigational skills. Persuasion, once known to orators and influencers, is now the lifeblood of effective digital marketing. It's the subtle art and science of influencing online behaviors, and it manifests itself in the six fundamental principles of persuasion: reciprocity, commitment and consistency, social proof, authority, liking, and scarcity. But knowing these principles is merely scratching the surface.

To truly harness the power of persuasion in the digital age, one must delve into the psyche of the digital consumer. It's crucial to understand the why before you can effectively manage the how. This book will be your compass, helping you decipher the map of digital consumer minds, and guiding you through conceiving strategies that leverage this knowledge for success.

Engagement in today's digital arena requires more than just attention-grabbing tactics. Marketers must develop an intimate understanding of their audience, defining personas that are as close to real customers as the data can predict. Just as a tailor measures twice to cut once, a successful digital strategy requires meticulous planning of the persuasion journey, ensuring each message resonates and compels action.

Content isn't just king; it's the emperor of all things digital. Understanding the role of content, from the written word to the moving image, is imperative. Mastery of content marketing enables you to educate, persuade, and leave lasting impressions. Through storytelling, blogs, and emails that convert, your message will be both the whisper and the shout in the ears of your audience.

The digital landscape is a canvas for creativity, and visuals are the colors with which marketers paint. Images and videos are not just assets; they are the language through which emotions and ideas are conveyed. Through understanding of visual persuasion, you can craft a visual impact that will magnify your message and its memorability.

No discussion on digital marketing would be complete without exploring the realm of social media. Each platform offers unique tools for creating community, fostering trust, and speaking the language of your target demographic. From the curated aesthetics of Instagram to the professional networks of LinkedIn, the ability to navigate these waters can make your strategic efforts all the more persuasive.

Visibility through search engines is a critical component of discovery. SEO and SEM are your beacons, guiding the vast online traffic to your digital doorstep. Crafting meta descriptions, titles, and understanding the subtleties of keyword intent are the latent forces behind being found in a crowded digital marketplace.

And in the age of big data, persuasion is married to analytics. The capacity to interpret data, to test and personalize, infuses your strategies with the precision of a craftsman. With A/B testing and personalization at your disposal, you finesse the art of persuasion into a science of impact.

Artificial intelligence is no longer a distant concept; it's here, reshaping the very fabric of our marketing tapestries. AI enables tailored experiences at scale, predictive analytics, and an unprecedented level of conversational marketing through technologies like chatbots. The future we imagined is now the present we live in.

Yet, amidst all this technological advancement, the human aspect of marketing remains pivotal. Influencer marketing and authentic collaborations can create resonance that technology alone cannot. These partnerships, when formed and nurtured correctly, offer humanity and authenticity in a domain often criticized for its lack of personal touch.

Equally significant is the concept of community—a cornerstone in the architecture of digital persuasion. In building engagement platforms, hosting live sessions, and fostering interactive content, you cultivate an environment for genuine connection and a space where your brand narrative can thrive.

As we embark on this journey together, let us remember that the digital revolution in marketing is more than technology—it's the story of connection, persuasion, and ultimately, it's about the meaningful relationships built between brands and their audiences. This book is not just a roadmap; it's your personal guide to navigating the waters of digital persuasion with confidence and creativity. Let's embrace the digital revolution with the intent not just to participate, but to lead the charge.

Chapter 1:
The Psychology of Persuasion

Mastering the subtle art of persuasion is like holding the keys to the digital kingdom, where the currency is attention and the throne is influence. In the realm of clicks, likes, and shares, understanding how to navigate the human psyche is paramount for anyone looking to flourish. It's an intricate dance between mind and heart, where leveraging well-established psychological principles can transform passive onlookers into active participants and loyal advocates. This chapter delves into the six fundamental principles that form the backbone of influence. It's here we unpack the reasoning why consumers say 'yes' and how you can ethically guide this response towards your digital offerings. Each principle, when adeptly integrated into your digital strategy, can elevate your brand above the cacophony of the online marketplace, creating experiences that resonate deeply and engender trust. Embrace these insights, and you'll not only captivate your audience but also inspire them to action - the ultimate triumph in the digital arena.

Understanding the Six Principles of Influence

In the arena of digital marketing, mastering the six principles of influence is akin to wielding a strategic roadmap for navigating the psychology of consumer behavior. As we craft our messaging and digital presence, understanding how Reciprocity can turn a casual browser into a loyal customer, or how Commitment and Consistency are essential in building a trustworthy brand narrative, is imperative. We delve into the power of Social Proof and how it amplifies credibility within online communities. The authority principle not only bolsters your brand's standing but also acts as a beacon for those seeking expert knowledge in your domain. From there, we harness the principle of Liking, acknowledging that relatability fosters profound connections with your audience, thereby enhancing your persuasive reach. Lastly, Scarcity isn't about withholding; it's an art, creating a compelling perceived value that engenders urgency and action. Embracing these principles isn't just a tactic; it's a transformative approach to engendering a magnetic digital persona that irresistibly draws your audience closer, guiding them seamlessly from curiosity to conversion.

Reciprocity and Your Digital Content

Weaving the principle of reciprocity into your digital content strategy builds a bridge of mutual benefit between your brand and its audience. In the digital realm, smothered by a relentless flow of information and advertisement, standing out requires a strategy that resonates on a human level. The psychology of persuasion highlights the power of reciprocity—the tendency to return a favor. When deploying this principle, it's crucial to be genuine, strategic, and consistent to foster trust and long-lasting relationships.

Let's begin by clearly understanding reciprocity: it's an unwritten social rule that encourages people to repay what another person has provided. In the context of digital content, you can think of reciprocity as providing value to your users in the hope—but not the expectation—of receiving something valuable in return, whether that's their attention, engagement, or business.

Creating content that offers real value is the cornerstone of this strategy. This value can take countless forms: informative blog posts, insightful e-books, helpful tutorials, or even entertaining videos. It's content that helps, educates, or enriches your audience without immediate reciprocation. The goal is to establish a positive brand image; you're planting seeds for future engagement.

When crafting digital content, each piece should be created with the audience's needs in mind. Analyze their challenges and aspirations. What can you offer that will truly impact them? How can your expertise or products serve as a solution? It could be as simple as a series of posts that answer common questions related to your industry or an in-depth guide that addresses a complex issue.

Timing and relevance are pivotal when applying reciprocity in your content. Your offerings should be timely and tackle topics that are currently impacting your audience. For instance, a tax firm might provide free resources on tax preparation as the fiscal year-end approaches. This timely assistance positions the firm as helpful and knowledgeable, increasing the likelihood that readers will turn to them for paid services.

An essential aspect to keep in mind is to avoid the immediate hard sell. Let the value that you've provided do the talking. Users are savvy; they can sense when content is a veiled sales pitch. Your audience's trust can be won by providing free value, with the understanding that not every interaction leads directly to a conversion.

Try offering your audience an unexpected bonus. This could be an additional eBook when they sign up for a webinar or a surprise discount code at the end of an educational video. Such gestures reinforce the feeling of receiving a gift rather than a transaction, which can encourage a deeper connection with your brand.

However, do bear in mind that reciprocity is not a one-off event, but a strategy for the long haul. Consistency in offering value will solidify your brand's reputation over time. Your audience will come to expect high-quality content from you, and their likelihood to reciprocate—in various forms—will increase.

User-generated content is another avenue where reciprocity can shine. By showcasing your customers' content, you're not only providing them with a platform but also implicitly thanking them for their loyalty. This acknowledgment often fuels further engagement and content generation from your user base.

Integration with social media is a natural step for reciprocity. Social sharing of impactful content can act as a method of users reciprocating the value they've received. Make sure your content is easily shareable, and encourage your audience to pass on the value to their own networks.

Influencer collaborations can also play a role in this strategy. When done authentically, leveraging influencers who can provide complementary value to your audience caters to the reciprocal nature of this digital marketing dynamic. The influencer gains content to share with their followers, while you gain access to a broader audience.

Keep a keen eye on feedback from your audience—what kind of content elicits the most positive response or engagement? Use these insights to refine your offerings further. The more you can align your content with audience interests, the stronger the reciprocal relationship will become.

Seeing reciprocity in action is truly impactful. For instance, maybe after utilizing your free resources, a follower invests in your paid course or recommends your services to friends. Each instance of reciprocation, whether big or small, reinforces the strength of your digital marketing efforts.

In deploying reciprocity, authenticity should never waver. Any attempt to game the system by creating a false veneer of value will be quickly seen through and can do lasting damage to your brand's reputation. Instead, commit to genuinely providing value and establishing a positive foundation for your audience to build upon.

As you continue to nourish the reciprocal relationship with your audience through valuable digital content, remember to measure the effectiveness of this strategy. Tracking engagement, leads, sales, and customer loyalty can all help in understanding how well reciprocity is working for you.

In conclusion, the power of reciprocity in your digital content is not just in the value that you provide, but in the ongoing, genuine relationship that you build with your audience. Maintain a commitment to value, track your results, and optimize your strategy. Through these efforts, you create a potent cycle of mutual benefit that drives both audience satisfaction and business success.

Commitment and Consistency in Brand Messaging

These are essential for creating a resilient brand identity that resonates deeply with your target audience. It's the steadfast dedication to a set of core messages, values, and visual elements over time, building a trustworthy relationship between brand and customer. This unwavering devotion is not merely about persistence; it's about nurturing a sense of familiarity and reliability that is compelling in its own right.

In our digitally-saturated world, consumers are bombarded with a multitude of messages every day. Amidst this chaos, consistency stands out as a beacon of familiarity that can lead to heightened brand recall and loyalty. When a brand consistently communicates its unique value proposition, story, and values across all platforms, customers are more likely to form a strong mental association with it.

Consider the principle of commitment, a potent psychological trigger in persuasion. When customers commit to your brand—

perhaps by signing up for your newsletter, following you on social media, or making a purchase—they're more likely to remain consistent with that decision if your brand reciprocates by maintaining consistency in what it stands for. This psychological alignment creates a bond that is not easily broken.

How does a brand ensure that it remains committed and consistent? It all starts with understanding your brand's essence. A crystal-clear grasp of who you are as a brand, what you stand for, and who you're speaking to form the foundation of consistent messaging. This isn't a one-and-done activity but a continuous effort that involves constantly revisiting and reaffirming these core principles.

A brand guide or style guide can be an invaluable tool in this endeavor. This document codifies your brand's voice, tone, visual guidelines, and core messaging tenets. Whether it's the color palette used in your visuals or the voice projected in your blog posts, a brand guide ensures everyone involved is singing from the same hymn sheet.

Consistent messaging also involves a nuanced understanding of your audience. You need to know their language, their struggles, and what keeps them up at night. This deep empathy allows you to craft messages that not only remain true to your brand's essence but also resonate on a personal level with your audience.

It's important to note that consistency doesn't mean the inertia of creativity. Rather, it's about innovating within the framework of your established brand identity. Whether it's a market shift requiring a new angle on your product or integrating new digital marketing tools into your strategy, these changes should still align with your core brand messaging.

Persistence in your digital marketing efforts plays a crucial role in actualizing commitment and consistency. Crafting an editorial calendar for content marketing, scheduling regular updates for social media, and planning steady email marketing campaigns are all tactics that anchor your brand's commitment to engaging your audience consistently.

Challenges will inevitably arise. Market dynamics change, new trends emerge, and competition intensifies. During these times, it is your commitment to brand consistency that will distinguish you. It'll necessitate agility within your operations – to embrace innovations and adapt to shifts without losing the essence of your brand messaging.

Data analytics can be a North Star in this process. By consistently monitoring how your audience interacts with your brand across multiple platforms, you can refine your messaging to ensure it remains relevant and effective. This approach dances the line between consistency and adaptability, responding to data-driven insights without eroding your brand's identity.

One cannot overstate the importance of employee alignment with your brand's values and messaging. When your team internalizes your brand's ethos, they will naturally express it through their work, whether it be in customer service, social media interactions, or content creation. In essence, your team becomes brand ambassadors imbued with the spirit of your brand.

Moreover, commitment and consistency should be reflected not just in what you say, but also in what you do. When your brand promises an exceptional customer experience, every touchpoint must deliver on that promise. When it touts sustainability, your operational choices must align. This integrity between messaging and action fosters authenticity, a currency of incalculable value in today's marketplace.

Remember, a brand that sways with every wind of trend and market pressure is like a ship without an anchor. It may float along the currents for a while, but it lacks direction and purpose. A commitment to consistent branding, conversely, is an anchor in unsteady waters, painting a clear picture for your customers about who you are and, importantly, why they should care.

In conclusion, the marriage of commitment and consistency is your brand's love letter to predictability—strategically and creatively deployed—in an unpredictable world. As you venture forth in your digital marketing endeavors, remember that consistency is the thread that weaves through each element of your brand's fabric, holding it together with strength and coherence. Let the constancy of your brand's messaging be the steady drumbeat that guides your quest for persuasion in the digital arena.

Let this truth sink in: people crave consistency as much as they yearn for breakthroughs. Your ability to provide both consistently and innovatively will be your brand's enduring legacy and the reason customers will return, time after time. Aim to make every interaction with your brand an affirmation of the commitment you uphold and the unwavering consistency that underscores your brand's every move.

Social Proof in Online Communities

In the interconnected tapestry of the digital marketplace, online communities have emerged as bustling hubs for brand interaction and customer engagement. Tapping into these vibrant ecosystems requires a shrewd understanding of social proof – a principle of influence that leverages the behavioral patterns within a group to bolster credibility and trust in a brand or product. In this digital era, leveraging social proof is not just an option; it's a linchpin for connecting with your audience and nurturing your brand's digital footprint.

Social proof takes many forms in online communities: customer testimonials, user reviews, social shares, and the visible endorsements of peers are just a few examples. This phenomenon is anchored in the basic human tendency to observe and emulate the behaviors of others, especially in situations where decisions are complex or uncertain. The weight of collective approval or disapproval in these communities can significantly shape consumer perceptions and actions.

The utilization of user-generated content (UGC) is a powerful form of social proof. When customers share their experiences with your brand on social media or forums, they're providing a candid endorsement that potential customers find relatable and trustworthy. These organic testimonials are digital marketing gold, as they resonate more authentically than any branded content ever could.

Influencer partnerships, while not entirely user-generated, also act as social proof by aligning your brand with trusted voices within the community. When an influencer speaks positively about your product, their followers—many of whom are part of your targeted online community—take note. This sense of approval from a respected member of the online tribe can drive engagement and conversions.

Recognition badges and affiliations can enhance your brand's standing in online communities as well. Displaying industry awards, certification seals, or partnership logos on your website and social media profiles indicates to community members that your brand has been vetted and endorsed by reputable entities. This form of recognized social proof adds a layer of professionalism and authenticity to your digital presence.

Customer reviews and star ratings on platforms specific to your industry or widely trusted review sites can immensely affect purchasing decisions. Encouraging satisfied customers to leave a review not only demonstrates confidence in your product or service but also builds a repository of positive social proof that can sway indecisive prospects in your favor.

Embracing social proof also means engaging directly with your online community. Promptly responding to questions, concerns, and feedback on social media and other digital platforms shows that your brand values customer input and is actively involved in the community. This level of engagement elevates your social proof by solidifying your brand's reputation as accessible and customer-centric.

Leveraging user statistics can further establish social proof. Sharing milestones such as the number of satisfied customers served, products sold, or subscribers gained, reflects the trust your brand has earned within the community. This quantitative evidence helps to subconsciously validate consumer choices in favor of your offerings.

Creating and cultivating brand ambassadors within online communities can amplify your brand's social proof. By identifying passionate customers who are willing to spread the word about your product or service, you create a pool of natural advocates. Their genuine enthusiasm becomes contagious, setting off a chain reaction of positive sentiment across the community.

Exclusive memberships or customer clubs can provide another level of social proof. When community members see others accessing special content, discounts, or events, it not only creates a feeling of FOMO (fear of missing out) but also signals that your brand is worth the commitment and loyalty.

Integrating social proof into product launches or updates can be particularly effective. By showcasing testimonials, user anticipation, or waiting lists, you convey the impression of high demand and product superiority. Nothing speaks louder than a queue of eager customers, ready to vouch for the next big thing from your brand.

In the vast universe of online communities, storytelling can enhance social proof by connecting the community through shared experiences. Narratives that highlight customer journeys, from problem to solution via your product, resonate deeply and contribute to the collective understanding and approval of your brand.

Keep in mind that quantity should not override quality. It's crucial to ensure that the social proof you demonstrate aligns with your brand values and resonates with your particular community. A hundred lukewarm testimonials cannot compare with a single, profoundly impactful customer story that strikes at the heart of communal challenges and aspirations.

Monitoring and managing your brand's social proof require continuous effort. Digital platforms are dynamic, with public opinion susceptible to swift changes. Regularly engaging with your audience, refreshing social proof with up-to-date content, and addressing any negative perceptions with tact and transparency are all part of maintaining the integrity of your social proof.

Finally, ethical considerations must not be overlooked in the pursuit of leveraging social proof. Authenticity is paramount; manipulating reviews, fabricating testimonials, or engaging in deceptive community engagement strategies can backfire and cause irreparable damage to your brand's reputation. Instead, focus on fostering genuine connections and providing exceptional experiences that naturally lead to positive social proof.

In conclusion, harnessing the potency of social proof in online communities demands a strategic approach that is both ethical and attuned to the nuances of digital interaction. By sincerely engaging with your audience, cultivating a positive presence, and showcasing the trust others have in your brand, you effectively underscore your digital authority and carve a persuasive path in the competitive market landscape.

Authority: Establishing Your Digital Domain

In the vast expanse of the digital realm, establishing authority is not just advantageous; it is imperative. Navigating this space requires a strong digital domain where your brand's expertise shines brightly, beckoning customers to trust in your services or products.

In the quest to build this essential facet of your online presence, it's critical to understand that authority is not self-assigned but rather earned through consistent efforts that validate your expertise and credibility. Establishing a digital domain where your brand can exert substantial influence involves multiple layers, each reinforcing your position as a leader in your industry.

To begin, the foundation of your authority is built upon high-quality content that speaks directly to the needs and desires of your target audience. This content, whether in the form of blog posts, white papers, or case studies, must not only provide value but should also be rooted in your unique insights and experiences. By delivering consistently excellent content, you not only inform your audience but also position yourself as a knowledgeable resource they can rely on.

Furthermore, a sophisticated website serves as your digital headquarters, lending credibility and professionalism to your brand. It's not just about aesthetics; functionality, navigation, and user experience are paramount in asserting your brand's competency. Your website should be a hub where valuable resources are easily accessible, and customer interactions can be nurtured towards a rapport of trust.

Another pillar in building authority is your active presence on relevant social media platforms. Here, consistency in brand messaging enforces the perception of a reliable and authoritative voice. However, it's not just about broadcasting messages; engaging with your audience, answering questions, and providing insights all help cement your standing as an authority figure within social spaces.

Behind the scenes, search engine optimization (SEO) is a silent yet potent driver of authority. By optimizing your digital content for search engines, you enhance visibility and demonstrate relevance in the eyes of both your audience and search algorithms. This inevitably results in higher rankings, which are often interpreted by users as markers of trustworthiness and authority.

Moreover, cultivating relationships with other reputable entities within your niche can broadcast a strong signal of authority. Partnering with or gaining endorsements from established influencers or trusted organizations within your field can significantly enhance your reputation and broaden your influence.

Then there is thought leadership. By being at the forefront of conversations about industry trends, innovations, or challenges, you not only shape discussions but also become the go-to resource for insights. This can be accomplished through speaking engagements, webinars, and participation in industry panels.

Awards and certifications have their role in the mosaic of authority as well. Achieving recognition from respected bodies within your industry not only boosts your profile but also serves as tangible proof of your expertise and commitment to quality.

Customer testimonials and case studies are powerful endorsements that give life to your claims of excellence. Sharing stories of success connects with prospective clients on an emotional level, reinforcing your authority through the satisfaction and triumphs of others.

However, authority can't be a surface-level veneer; it needs to be infused throughout every customer interaction. From the attentiveness shown in customer service to the after-sales support, all reinforce the idea that your brand is a reliable authority that cares about customer experience.

It's crucial, too, to stay abreast of the latest industry developments and technological advancements. Lifelong learning and adaptability communicate to your audience that you are an ever-evolving authority, capable of steering them through the changing tides of the marketplace.

Indeed, protecting your digital reputation is paramount. Your online reviews and social media mentions are visible indicators of your brand's authority. Promptly addressing concerns and maintaining a positive digital footprint is essential in upholding your authoritative status.

To amplify authority, wield data-driven insights that tailor your messaging and approach. By illustrating an understanding of your audience's behaviors and preferences, you reassert your position as a well-informed leader equipped to cater to their specific needs.

Lastly, never underestimate the power of a consistent narrative. Your brand's story should weave through every piece of content, every interaction, and every strategy, reinforcing the core values and mission that set you apart.

Authority in your digital domain is not established overnight but emerges as a byproduct of dedication to excellence, a strategic approach to online interactions, and an unwavering commitment to providing value. It's an ongoing journey, one that requires vigilance, agility, and an unyielding quest to serve your audience at the highest level.

Liking: The Power of Relatability

As we navigate the digital landscape, one principle of influence stands as a universal connector between brand and consumer—liking. The age-old adage that people do business with those they know, like, and trust still resonates deeply in the virtual world. However, the mechanism behind this simple observation is rooted in a powerful psychological underpinning: relatability. When you manage to bridge the gap between your brand and your audience, you not only spark engagement but also open the door for lasting loyalty.

Liking isn't merely about being pleasant or agreeable. It's about finding and accentuating common ground, shared values, and mutual understanding with your audience. To harness the power of relatability, you must first understand your audience on a granular level. This involves deep, insightful research into their interests, challenges, desires, and pain points. Once armed with this knowledge, drawing parallels between their world and what your brand stands for becomes a strategic endeavor.

The digital era has provided an arena where authenticity reigns supreme. Users are constantly bombarded with content, making it critical for brands to communicate in a way that feels genuine and transparent. This authenticity engenders a sense of familiarity. As a byproduct, your audience begins to develop a subconscious affinity towards your brand. To convey authenticity, let your brand's unique personality shine through every interaction, whether it's a social media post, email, or blog article.

Storytelling is a formidable tool in the arsenal of relatability. A compelling narrative can transport your audience through a journey where they see themselves reflected in your brand's story. By deploying storytelling across your digital channels, you can paint a picture that feels both personal and universal, easing the process of identification with your brand's values and mission.

Relatability also comes from consistency. Your brand's voice should be unchanging across all platforms; it should be a voice that your audience can become familiar with, no matter where they encounter you. When your messaging is consistent, your audience feels like they are in a stable relationship. This strengthened sense of familiarity contributes to the 'liking' factor.

Interactive content such as quizzes, polls, and surveys can serve as excellent tools for promoting relatability. By inviting your audience to participate, you not only engage them but also learn more about them, thereby shaping your content to better fit their preferences. As a result, they'll see your brand as more attentive and tailored to their needs, thus becoming more relatable.

Visuals should not be overlooked when striving for relatability. Using images and videos that your audience can identify with helps in solidifying your message. Represent your audience within your brand's visuals, and you'll make them feel seen and understood. Humanizing your brand with visuals showing real people, real emotions, and real situations acts as a fast track to creating a connection.

User-generated content (UGC) can amplify the relatability factor immensely. Featuring content created by your audience not only endorses it as valuable but also legitimizes the experiences of your consumers with your brand. This peer validation is a potent form of social proof that naturally enhances the likability of your brand.

Engagement is the currency of the digital world, and having meaningful interactions with your audience is a surefire way to heighten relatability. Don't just broadcast; create dialogues. Respond to comments, acknowledge feedback, and address concerns with a personal touch. Show that there are real people behind the brand who care and can relate to their audience's perspectives.

One of the nuanced aspects of 'liking' is leveraging shared experiences or challenges. In moments of universal hardship (such as during a global pandemic), showing solidarity, empathy, and support can significantly boost your brand's relatability. Sharing how your brand understands and is working to improve the situation resonates with the collective consciousness of your audience.

Inclusion and diversity are also critical factors in building a likable and relatable brand. By embracing a spectrum of voices, backgrounds, and experiences within your brand's representation, you're sending a message that everyone is welcome. This level of acceptance is attractive to audiences who seek to be part of communities that value inclusivity.

Aligning with causes that resonate with your audience further enhances relatability. This shows your brand takes a stand on issues beyond your products or services and that you're committed to the values you share with your audience. Cause marketing, when done with sincerity, can transform a business entity into a beloved brand that people are proud to associate with.

Remember, in the pursuit of likability, it's crucial to remain true to your brand's core identity. Authenticity should not be sacrificed on the altar of relatability; the two must coexist in harmony. When you are true to your brand's values while making a concerted effort to understand and mirror your audience's values, a natural alignment occurs, engendering genuine likability.

Finally, never underestimate the power of humor. When used appropriately, humor can break barriers, make your brand approachable, and create memorable experiences. Humor is a shared aspect of humanity, and when it resonates with your audience, it can make your brand instantly more likeable. However, tread carefully and ensure that your brand's humor aligns with your audience's sensitivity and taste.

In conclusion, leveraging likability through relatability is a multifaceted strategy that involves deep audience insight, storytelling, visual and interactive content, social proof, engagement, shared values, inclusivity, and a dash of humor. It's an art that appeals to the heart—by being genuinely relatable, you create a magnetic force that cannot only attract but also retain customers, turning them into advocates for your brand. Cultivate likability, and watch as the power of relatability transforms your digital marketing efforts into a symphony of persuasion that resonates with the core of your audience.

Scarcity: Creating Perceived Value Online

Harnessing the power of scarcity transforms products into coveted prizes, driving consumers to action out of fear of missing out. Scarcity breeds a sense of urgency, compelling users to seize offerings before they slip away. In the vast expanse of the internet, manufacturing this urgency aligns with art, requiring a deft touch, shrewd timing, and the understanding of your audience's deepest desires.

Begin by assessing your product or service's unique proposition and how it stands in the market. Is it a limited edition Offering? Could it be positioned as a seasonal must-have? Identifying a legitimate scarcity vector provides a solid foundation for your campaign. Artificial scarcity can resonate as disingenuous, so the key is finding real value in limited availability.

Launching a pre-order campaign is an exemplary tactic to spotlight the exclusivity of your new product. It's simple psychology; if people can't have it yet, they want it more. Illuminate the benefits of early-bird privileges, such as discounted rates or exclusive access, to instill a sense of priority among your consumers and a fear of missing out. Introduce a countdown timer on your website or landing pages. This ticking clock is not just a visual cue but an auditory one too, even in its silence – a constant reminder that time, and by extension the offer, is running out.

Communicate scarcity through your messaging. Crafting email campaigns that emphasize a limited time offer not only captivates attention but also propels action. Subject lines with phrases like "Last Chance!" or "While Supplies Last" work wonders because they're clear and create instant urgency. Sprinkle these messages throughout your social media, ensuring consistency across all digital touchpoints.

Consider leveraging partnerships for exclusive releases. Collaborations with influencers or other brands can infuse your product with an aura of exclusivity and attractiveness that scarcity naturally bestows. Remember, perceived rarity increases the value – it's the fundamental rule of the scarcity principle.

Flash sales are another dynamic method to induce scarcity. The brevity of the sale period spurs people into action. Digital marketers can leverage social media stories, which by their disappearing nature, echo the ephemeral nature of such sales, reinforcing the 'act now' urgency.

But don't forget – scarcity needs social proof to fully thrive. Displaying real-time stock levels or a customer count can press the urgency: "Only 3 left and 15 people have this in their cart!" is a powerful motivator. It's a visualization of demand that creates a magnetic pull for the undecided shopper.

Product differentiation also falls under scarcity's purview. By highlighting the unique features of a product or service, its scarcity becomes self-evident. Maybe it's a handcrafted item, or perhaps it's built with unparalleled material – underline these aspects to emphasize scarcity.

Subscription models can also play on scarcity. Offering exclusive content or products to subscribers introduces a gated community effect. It's about belonging to an elite group with access to what others can't have, stirring a desire for inclusion that prompts sign-ups.

Be mindful; scarcity must never cross into manipulation. Transparency is key. Ensure that your scarcity marketing aligns with truthful supply dynamics. Misleading customers may yield short-term gains, but it damages brand trust in the long run.

Data is also your ally in executing scarcity strategies. Use analytics to understand the optimal timing for scarcity campaigns and measure engagement to tweak and tailor your methods. The goal is to create genuine urgency without resorting to pressure tactics.

An often-overlooked aspect of scarcity is customer follow-up. After the scarcity-triggered purchase, nurture the relationship. Reassure customers of their wise decision, and you will instill loyalty that extends far beyond the urgent click of a "Buy Now" button.

Finally, remember even in scarcity, the customer journey matters. A user's frantic push to claim an offer can lead to a negative experience if not handled with care. Streamline the purchasing process, provide ample customer support, and reassure users — even amidst the rush — that their satisfaction is paramount.

To sum it up, effective scarcity taps into a human instinct – the desire to obtain what is hard to come by. In the digital marketplace, this can be a game-changer. By strategically applying scarcity to your online endeavors, you enhance the intrinsic value of your offerings. Just remember to pair scarcity with integrity, and your brand will not only enjoy a boost in urgency-induced sales but also in steadfast customer loyalty and trust.

Chapter 2:
Crafting Your Digital Persuasion Strategy

In this digital era, crafting an effective persuasion strategy is more than just capturing attention—it's about creating meaningful connections. As we delve into the heart of digital persuasion, we'll establish the bedrock of this strategy: knowing your audience intimately. Who are they? What do they yearn for? How do they navigate the ever-shifting online landscape? With each swipe, click, and interaction, your audience is signaling their needs and preferences, paving the way for a powerful digital persuasion journey. In this chapter, we're setting the stage for a symphony of interactions across multiple channels, orchestrated to resonate with your audience's core desires and motivations. Each touchpoint is a note in the broader melody of your brand's narrative, played across the intricate network of the digital realm. Mastering this symphony is how you turn casual browsers into loyal advocates, and in doing so, achieve a level of influence that transforms your online presence into a beacon of persuasion. As the digital tapestry unfolds, your message needs to be cohesive, your approach adaptive, and your strategy clear. Let the crafting begin.

Defining Your Target Audience in the Digital Space

Diving into the digital realm without a clear understanding of your audience is akin to setting sail without a compass. The quest to resonate with a potential customer, influence their decision-making, and ultimately persuade them to take action begins with a profoundly simple step: defining your target audience in the digital space. This process is both an art and a science, requiring a deep dive into analytics, psychology, and market trends.

The foundational element of any digital persuasion strategy is laying out a blueprint of whom you are trying to reach. Are they tech-savvy millennials with an affinity for sustainable brands or are they budget-conscious parents searching for the best deals online? The granularity with which you outline your audience's demographics, psychographics, behaviors, and online habits will dictate the precision of your digital marketing efforts.

To pinpoint your audience, start with data — both the qualitative and quantitative kinds. Analytics tools can provide you with rich insights about the users interacting with your digital properties. But don't overlook the wealth of knowledge that can be garnered from real conversations with customers, surveys, and social media engagement.

Every digital interaction is a gold mine of information. Leverage the power of social listening to understand the topics and issues that resonate with your audience. This isn't eavesdropping; it's an essential part of your strategy to ensure that your message hits home. Social platforms hold the key to understanding public perception and the prevailing sentiments among your prospective buyers.

Once you have a grip on the 'who,' it's essential to fathom the 'why.' Why do they choose to engage online? Are they seeking information, entertainment, social connection, or maybe a mix of all three? Understanding their motivations will allow you to craft messages that tap into these intrinsic desires.

Personas are more than compilations of characteristics; they are the embodiment of the audience you aim to persuade. Create detailed personas to humanize your data. Give them names, backstories, and potential pain points. This will enable you to approach your audience with empathy and create digital experiences that feel personal and relatable.

Mapping out your audience's digital habits is crucial. Which platforms do they frequent? Are they scrolling through Instagram, searching on Google, or networking on LinkedIn? Each channel has its unique nuances, and your message needs to be tailored to align with the context and the expectations of the audience within each space.

Remember, defining your audience is not a 'one and done' task. As the digital landscape evolves, so do user preferences and behaviors. Regularly reassess and refine your target audience based on the latest data and trends. Being adaptive in this way ensures that your persuasion strategy remains potent and relevant.

One of the most powerful tools in your digital arsenal is segmentation. By dividing your audience into subgroups based on certain criteria, you can tailor your messaging to speak to specific interests, circumstances, or pain points. This not only enhances relevance but also significantly increases the likelihood of a positive response.

Contextual relevance cannot be overstated. It can mean the difference between a message that is embraced and one that is ignored. Your data analysis and audience definition should guide you in determining when and where to place your content for maximum effect. Timing, platform choice, and message framing should all be delicately balanced to ensure your audience feels understood, not just targeted.

Audience definition also involves understanding the journey your customers take to reach you, but don't confuse this journey mapping with the next step—each is a vital, distinct phase in your digital persuasion strategy. In this phase, focus on the audience's starting point, their pain points, their information sources, and other influencing factors in their environment.

Lastly, keep in mind that in the digital space, competition for attention is fierce. Your competitors are also vying to define and appeal to a similar target audience. Conduct a thorough competitive analysis to see how others are crafting their persuasive strategies and look for gaps you can fill or advantages you can leverage.

In essence, defining your target audience is akin to setting the coordinates for your journey through the digital landscape. With these coordinates firmly in place, you are better equipped to navigate the vast and tumultuous waters of digital marketing. The result is a persuasive strategy that is not just heard but listened to, not just seen but observed, and ultimately, not just presented but felt by the very people you aim to engage and inspire.

Remember, the resonance of your digital strategy is directly proportional to the clarity of your audience definition. So, invest the time to get to know your audience intimately. The depth of connection you achieve can turn potential customers into loyal advocates, and therein lies the true power of digital persuasion well executed.

With your target audience now meticulously defined and etched in your strategy, you're ready to carve the pathways that will guide them towards the actions you want them to take. The subsequent sections will build upon this foundation, ensuring that your digital persuasion strategy doesn't just cast a wide net, but rather, entices the right fish into swimming straight into it.

Mapping the Persuasion Journey

The pathway to effectively persuading your online audience involves much more than compelling content; it requires a deep understanding of the journey your prospects embark on from initial exposure to the final action. This persuasion journey is critical to crafting a digital strategy that converts, resonates, and sustains long-term engagement.

Start by envisioning the digital landscape as a vast sea, your audience as voyagers, and your brand as the beacon guiding them to the desired destination. Consider each touchpoint on this journey an opportunity for you to illuminate their path, build trust, and ultimately, persuade them to take the action you want.

Firstly, identify the starting point where your audience encounters your brand. Is it a social media post, a search engine result, or a banner ad on a partner website? This initial contact is the crucial spark that sets the journey in motion. Ensure this touchpoint is impactful and aligns seamlessly with what follows; consistency breeds comfort and trust, leading to smoother sailing ahead.

Next, chart out the subsequent steps your audience will take after the first encounter. Will they click through to your website, sign up for a newsletter, or watch a demonstration video? Your audience's actions must flow naturally from one to the next, avoiding any jarring transitions that could cause them to abandon ship.

Once the sequence of steps is plotted, inject your unique brand personality into each stage. Remember, the journey should be enjoyable and informative. Use your digital presence to assure them they're in capable hands. This is where persuasive techniques tailored to digital media come into play.

Persuading someone doesn't happen in a vacuum; it happens within the context of a relationship. Nurture this relationship by presenting valuable and relevant content at each stage. A comprehensive understanding of the six principles of influence outlined in Chapter 1 will guide you to be strategic in shaping these interactions.

Throughout the journey, leverage the principle of reciprocity. Provide your audience with resources and benefits for free. This could mean offering insightful articles, helpful e-books, or exclusive access to webinars. This builds goodwill and increases their likelihood of reciprocating with the behavior you're seeking, such as making a purchase or sharing your content.

As you guide your audience along, reinforce the commitment and consistency you've established. Stay true to your brand's message, and use every communication to solidify the audience's understanding of who you are and what you stand for. Consistent messaging reinforces your brand's identity and reinforces the persuasive subtleties you've woven into your content.

Moreover, infuse social proof throughout the journey. Display testimonials, user-generated content, and success stories to show your prospects they're not the first to navigate this path. Knowing others have successfully made it to the destination increases their confidence and propels them forward.

Cement your authority by demonstrating expertise and credibility at every twist and turn. Use data-backed insights, case studies, and expert opinions to fortify the trust they've placed in you. This trust places you in an advantageous position of influence.

Keep the journey personal and humanized by embracing 'liking.' Craft your messaging in a way that resonates on a personal level; use language and visuals that reflect your audience's preferences and attitudes. A brand that's relatable is like a friend who's guiding the way, making persuasion feel like a natural outcome of a valued relationship.

And as your prospects move closer to the journey's end, remind them, subtly, of what's at stake. Utilize scarcity by highlighting limited-time offers, exclusivity, or the potential loss of opportunity if they don't act. This sense of urgency should nudge them towards conversion, not out of fear but out of a desire not to miss out on something special.

Remember, the persuasion journey doesn't end at the first conversion—it's a continuous loop. Keep mapping out new journeys with different destinations for your existing customers. Retention is key, and by continuously engaging and persuading through an ongoing narrative, you not only keep your audience-captivated but turn them into brand ambassadors, echoing your messaging into uncharted territories of the digital sea.

Effective mapping of the persuasion journey allows you to spot potential barriers that could derail your prospects. Anticipate these obstacles ahead of time and have strategies in place to address them. A dynamic map that responds to real-time feedback from analytics provides the agility to navigate the ever-changing digital waters effectively.

Your ability to lead and persuade in the digital space is not static—it's a carefully curated process that adapts, evolves, and refines as your understanding of your audience deepens. Just like a seasoned captain at the helm, be prepared to weather storms, chart new courses, and discover unexplored territories with your audience by your side. Successful digital persuasion is about providing a journey that's as rewarding as the destination itself.

Integrating Multiple Channels for Cohesive Messaging

In an era brimming with digital channels, a strategy that articulates a singular, clear message across this diverse landscape isn't just ideal—it's paramount. As we delve into the concept of integrating multiple channels for cohesive messaging, we recognize the powerful synergy that occurs when different forms of media work in concert, reinforcing and amplifying the same message in a harmonized digital symphony.

Picture each digital channel as a musician in an orchestra—social media, email, blogging, video channels, all poised with unique instruments. Played solo, each resonates with its own charm. However, when orchestrated together under a single baton, the resulting melody can move audiences, drive engagement, and influence behavior. That's the essence of cohesive messaging: crafting an experience that feels seamlessly connected and relentlessly focused on delivering value to the audience.

Begin with a consistent narrative that aligns with your brand's core values and mission. This narrative should be the golden thread weaving through all forms of communication. When someone jumps from your Instagram stories to your blog, and then to an email newsletter, the continuity of that narrative reassures them of your brand's consistency and relatability. It's this repeated reinforcement that fosters trust and propels your audience further along the persuasion journey.

But consistency shouldn't be mistaken for replication. Adapting the message appropriately to fit the context of each channel is vital. While the overarching message remains steady, its presentation needs to be channel-specific. An infographic for LinkedIn, a platform with a professional audience, should be more data-driven and formal compared to an Instagram post, which may be more visual and casual, yet both should be unmistakable siblings in the larger brand family.

Timing and content curation play crucial roles in messaging integration. Orchestrating simultaneous launches of cross-channel campaigns has the potential to create high-impact waves that ripple across the digital space. This simultaneous push ensures your message is unavoidable, engaging potential customers across multiple touchpoints.

Engagement is not a passive affair. To integrate channels effectively, you must actively listen and respond across all platforms.

When a comment is made under a promotional video on YouTube, it should be engaged with just as thoughtfully as a query on Twitter. This kind of attentive interaction showcases a unified and attentive brand ready to engage with its audience wherever they are.

Data is your compass when navigating the multi-channel seas. Leveraging analytics allows you to understand how messages resonate differently across channels. By tracking engagement metrics, click-through rates, and conversion data, you begin to paint a picture of where your strategies shine and where adjustments are needed.

With data in hand, segmentation becomes an essential ally. Not all of your audience will be present on all channels, and not all require the same approach. By segmenting your audience based on channel preferences, demographics, and behavior, you can tailor your messaging to echo the nuances of each group, ensuring relevance and impact.

Emerging trends should never be ignored in digital marketing. As new channels arise, they too must be knit into the fabric of your strategy. However, it's crucial to stay mindful of which channels make sense for your brand and message. Adopting a new platform because it's en vogue might lead to a disharmonious note in your orchestra if it doesn't resonate with your target audience.

Crisis management is an often-overlooked aspect of multi-channel integration. In times of brand crisis, having a uniform message across channels is fundamental. A misstep or inconsistent response can be amplified in the digital age, so prepare crisis communication plans that integrate all channels for quick and unified addressing of any issues that arise.

Test, learn, and optimize. The digital landscape is constantly shifting, and staying agile is key. A/B testing different messages across various channels can provide a wealth of insights into what approaches spark the most engagement and conversion. Through iterative testing, you're more equipped to sharpen the cutting edge of your digital persuasion strategy.

Do not forget the power of visual consistency. Ensuring that your visual branding is consistent across channels fortifies the recognizability of your messaging. Whether it's a color scheme, logo placement, or a style of imagery, these visual cues signal to your audience that they are within your branded digital space, no matter the platform.

While maintaining a strong integrated strategy, be wary of spreading too thin. It's better to be masterfully present on a few key channels than to be weakly represented on many. Choose your digital platforms based on where they best align with your goals and where your audience is most active, rather than trying to be everywhere all at once.

Last but certainly not least, remember the importance of content quality. Even the most well-integrated strategy will falter if the content doesn't resonate or provide value. Strive for materials that educate, inspire, entertain, or solve problems. Content that makes lives better travels furthest, reinforcing your brand's message with each share.

As we close this chapter on integrated multiple channels for coherent messaging, hold close the vision of your brand's narrative echoing across the vast digital expanse. It's a tale that informs, connects, and persuades, conveyed through a fine-tuned alignment of the many instruments at your disposal—channels, data, visuals, and content—all playing in unison with the single aim of winning hearts and minds, one message at a time.

Chapter 3:
The Written Word: Content Marketing Mastery

In the preceding chapters, we refined our understanding of the psychological underpinnings of persuasion and began to forge our digital persuasion strategy. Now, let's delve into the heartbeat of digital communication: the written word. Content marketing is the art and science of connecting with your audience through the purposeful creation and distribution of valuable content. Masters of this domain understand that it isn't just about producing content; it's about crafting messages that resonate deeply, enlighten, and galvanize the reader into action. From blogging to email campaigns, tapping into the art of storytelling will transform your narrative into an immersive journey for your audience. Each word you curate should be poised to reinforce the persuasive scaffolding you've meticulously constructed, ensuring that with every sentence read, your audience feels increasingly aligned with your vision and primed for the call to action that awaits.

Blogging: Educating and Persuading Your Audience

The art of blogging is a cornerstone in the realm of content marketing. It's an arena where words can inform, influence, and inspire action. As a digital marketer, professional, or entrepreneur, your mission is to harness the subtleties of language to engage a discerning audience and persuade them to embrace your narrative.

First, it is crucial to understand the framework of effective blogging—it begins with educational content. Education is the groundwork for persuasion. When you educate your audience, you're not merely transferring knowledge; you're building the foundation for trust. A well-informed reader is empowered to make decisions based on the understanding you've provided.

Succeeding in educating your readers requires you to align your content with their interests and challenges. Before you start crafting your posts, delve deep into the psyche of your target demographic. What are their pain points? What solutions are they seeking? An educational blog post must answer these questions and position your product or service as the logical next step in their quest for answers.

To ensure your educational content is persuasive, it must also captivate. This is where storytelling weaves its magic. Humans are inherently drawn to stories - they are the threads that connect us to unfamiliar ideas. A blog post that recounts a relatable experience or an inspirational journey can serve as a powerful vehicle for conveying your message.

An effective blog also utilizes the principles of influence outlined in your arsenal of persuasion techniques. When you provide valuable information freely, you ignite the principle of reciproactivity—your audience is naturally inclined to reciprocate the value they've received. This could manifest as sharing your content, subscribing to your list, or even purchasing your offerings.

A key aspect of blogging is consistency. This doesn't only pertain to the frequency of your posts but also to the tone, style, and message. Consistent blog content fortifies your brand's voice and reinforces your message. Over time, this consistency fosters trust, and trust is the currency of persuasion.

Social proof is another lever in the blogging machine that can escalate your persuasive power. Integrate reviews, testimonials, and case studies into your blog posts to showcase the trust others have put in your brand. Authentic narratives from satisfied customers or respected industry figures act as endorsements, subtly coaxing your audience toward your point of view.

When we talk about authority in blogging, we refer to demonstrating expertise. Blogs are an excellent platform to showcase your mastery. By producing insightful, well-researched content, you cement your brand's status as an industry leader. Readers are more likely to be persuaded by those who demonstrate their expertise with conviction.

The principle of liking suggests that people are more easily persuaded by those they like. Therefore, your blog must exude a personality that's relatable and likable. A conversational tone, personal anecdotes, or a touch of humor can endear you to your readers, making the persuasion process more fluid and natural.

Intelligently orchestrated scarcity can also come into play in your blogs. Limited-time offers or exclusive content can spur your audience into action. This, however, must be done with tact to avoid undermining the educational value of your content.

The structural integrity of your blog posts further strengthens your persuasive intent. Start with a compelling headline that piques interest. Follow with a hook—an opening that grabs attention and promises value. Then layout your content in digestible sections, using headlines and bullet points to enhance readability and retention.

Remember to incorporate a clear call-to-action (CTA) in every blog post. After educating and persuading, you must guide your audience to the next step. Whether it's to sign up for more information, download a guide, or make a purchase, the CTA is your moment to convert readership into action.

Amid the tactical execution of your blog posts, authenticity must be the beacon that guides your content. Persuasion should be rooted in genuine intent. Your audience can discern the difference between manipulation and meaningful engagement. Stay true to your brand values, and let that integrity shine through every post.

Measurement and refinement close the circle of blogging success. Utilize analytics to track the performance of your posts. Which topics resonate most with your audience? What type of content generates the highest engagement or leads to conversions? Leverage this data to fine-tune your approach continuously.

In conclusion, blogging is a dynamic instrument in your content marketing symphony. It's not just about writing; it's about weaving together education, persuasion, and influence to create a compelling narrative that resonates with your audience. Through consistent, authentic, and strategic blogging, you can educate your readers, shape their perceptions, and lead them confidently towards the actions that serve your marketing objectives. This is the mastery of the written word in the digital space—a mastery that fuses art with strategic intent to foster meaningful connections and drive results.

Email Strategies That Convert

Excelling in the digital arena demands mastery of numerous content marketing tools, and among the most potent is email marketing. Emails, when crafted with precision and understanding, are not just messages; they are keys to unlock the hidden potential of customer relationships and drive tangible conversions. Forging these keys correctly, however, requires a blend of art and science that digital marketers, professionals, and entrepreneurs must master to thrive.

Initiating our discourse, let's address the critical importance of understanding your audience. Segmenting your email list enables you to tailor your messages to specific subsets of your audience, ensuring relevance and increasing the likelihood of engagement. Personalization goes beyond adding a recipient's name; it involves delivering content that resonates with their individual needs, interests, and behaviors. This deep level of personalization cultivates a sense of uniqueness in the recipients' minds, making them feel valued and understood.

The subject line of any email serves as the gatekeeper. It determines whether your message is opened or condemned to the abyss of the unread. Crafting subject lines that intrigue and ignite curiosity can skyrocket your open rates. Keep them concise, compelling, and aligned with the content of your email to maintain trust and credibility. Test various subject lines to see what resonates with your audience and use the data to inform future strategies.

Within the body of your email, clarity and conciseness are essential. Your audience is besieged with information and distractions, so your content must cut through the noise. Construct a narrative that carries them through your email, imbuing each line with value and purpose. The use of compelling hooks and a conversational tone aids in maintaining the reader's interest and propels them towards action.

Call-to-action (CTA) is the directing force in your email that tells your audience precisely what you want them to do next. A compelling CTA is clear, urgent, and persuasive without being pushy. It stands out visually, often with a button or a distinct color, and is strategically placed to guide the reader's journey through the email. Ensure your CTA aligns with the value proposition outlined in your message for optimal impact.

Visuals can enhance the appeal and comprehension of your email content. While images should be used judiciously to preserve load times and avoid overwhelming readers, the right image can convey messages that words alone cannot. They support your storytelling, break up text, and add a dynamic element that contributes to the overall engagement of the email.

Establishing a rhythm with your email campaigns creates anticipation among your subscribers. Consistent delivery schedules and recurring themes can help to build habits and expectations, making your emails an awaited event rather than a random interruption. This timing strategy not only sustains engagement but also aids in constructing a reliable brand image in the eyes of your readers.

The power of storytelling in email marketing cannot be understated. Narratives create emotional connections with audiences, allowing you to weave your product or service into a larger, more relatable context. Share customer testimonials, success stories, and behind-the-scenes peeks to humanize your brand and illustrate the real-world value of your offerings.

A/B testing is an analytical approach to fine-tuning your email strategies. By experimenting with different versions of subject lines, email copy, images, and CTAs, you can discern what resonates most with your audience. This data-driven method helps in making informed decisions to optimize your email campaigns for better conversion rates.

Responsive design is non-negotiable in the current digital age. With a significant portion of emails being opened on mobile devices, your emails must be easily readable and interactable across all platforms. This seamless experience across devices enhances accessibility and reduces the friction that might prevent an interested reader from taking action.

Automation has revolutionized the way we approach email marketing. Triggered emails based on user behavior, such as abandoned cart messages and welcome sequences, allow for timely and relevant interaction with your audience. These automated sequences nurture leads and gently guide them down the conversion funnel, significantly boosting efficiency and effectiveness.

To maintain the integrity of your email campaigns, always prioritize compliance with regulations such as GDPR. Respect for privacy and consent not only adheres to legal standards but also garners respect from your audience, contributing to a foundation of trust that is imperative for a successful digital relationship.

After executing your strategies, the cycle does not end. Continuous monitoring and analysis are crucial. By closely observing open rates, click-through rates, and conversion metrics, you can keep your finger on the pulse of your campaign's vitality. These insights enable you to iterate and evolve your approach, staying ahead in a landscape that is perpetually changing.

Email marketing synergy with other digital channels amplifies its effectiveness. Incorporate social proof by sharing user-generated content, align blog content with email topics for consistency, and ensure that all digital touchpoints lead back to a cohesive message and brand voice. The integration of multiple channels reinforces your digital persuasion strategy from every angle.

The world of email marketing is one of nuance and continual learning. By implementing these strategies with diligence, creativity, and a steadfast commitment to understanding and resonating with your audience, remarkable conversions are not just possible – they're within reach. Embrace the challenge, nurture your craft, and watch as your emails become a compelling chapter in your brand's success story.

The Art of Storytelling in Digital Campaigns

In the realm of digital marketing, the ancient craft of storytelling has not lost its relevance; if anything, it has found a new playground. Stories captivate us, drive us to action, and leave lingering impressions that can last far longer than any fleeting advertisement. Within the digital vortex of content, a well-crafted story can be the beacon that captures an audience's attention and guides them towards engagement and loyalty. Precisely crafted storytelling can transform a mere product into a character in the user's life narrative, ultimately contributing to a brand's enduring success.

But why are stories so influential in digital campaigns? Human brains are hardwired for narrative. They seek connections and coherence amongst chaos, making stories an ideal vehicle for communication. In the context of digital marketing, storytelling translates complex offers into relatable experiences, creates emotional connections, and enhances memorability of the message.

Consider the journey of a story within a digital campaign. It begins with establishing a connection, typically through a relatable protagonist or situation. This is both an art and a science, entailing a deep understanding of the audience. Who are they? What are their challenges, desires, and dreams? The answers help tailor a narrative that resonates on a personal level, transforming the abstract into the accessible.

Effective storytelling in digital campaigns requires a keen sense of structure. Like any compelling novel or film, the story should have a clear beginning, middle, and end. It should introduce a conflict or challenge, provide a journey with the brand as an ally, and conclude with a resolution, ideally featuring the product as the hero that leads to a positive outcome. This arc is not only engaging but also helps the audience understand and remember the value proposition.

To weave such stories into a digital landscape, content must be adaptable across various platforms. Whether it's a blog, a social media post, or a web banner, the essence of the story should be consistent even as it's customized for the unique features and audiences of each channel. This creates a coherent brand narrative that consumers can follow regardless of where they engage with the campaign.

Emotion is the undercurrent of influential storytelling. Evoking emotions—whether it's joy, surprise, sadness, or awe—makes the message more impactful. Emotional stories not only increase engagement but also foster brand loyalty and advocacy. When a narrative makes us feel, we are more inclined to share that experience with others, creating an organic ripple effect of brand exposure.

However, in digital storytelling, authenticity cannot be overlooked. With a discerning audience that is bombarded with content endlessly, authenticity stands out. Brands that tell genuine stories that align with their values and vision not only capture attention but also build trust with their audience. Authenticity becomes the bedrock upon which long-term relationships are built.

Data can serve as a powerful tool in crafting your story. By analyzing audience behavior and preferences, you can refine your narrative to make it more relatable and engaging. Tracking how users respond to different story elements can inform future campaigns, making data an invaluable partner in the storytelling process.

Visual elements in storytelling are just as important as the narrative itself. They provide context, emphasize key messages, and make stories more captivating. The rise of visual platforms has made this more pertinent than ever. A single image can convey a whole chapter of emotion, making it essential for digital marketers to master visual storytelling alongside written content.

Interactivity can also elevate digital storytelling. By making the audience a part of the narrative—through choices, gamified elements, or simply immersive experiences—brands can deepen the engagement and make the story even more memorable. Moreover, such interactive stories provide valuable feedback about audience preferences and behaviors.

One must not forget the potency of simplicity in a digital narrative. Simplicity aids in clarity and helps the core message to shine through amid the cacophony of the digital space. The story should be easy to follow, regardless of the complexity of the product or service being offered. Consumers appreciate and are drawn to simplicity, which can lead to more profound engagement and conviction.

Storytelling is not merely a tool; it is an ongoing strategy that can evolve with the brand. It requires constant nurturing, innovation, and alignment with changing consumer sentiments. As brands grow, so should their stories, adapting and evolving to ensure they remain relevant and resonant within the hearts and minds of their audience.

The synergy of storytelling and technology presents an unrivaled opportunity for digital marketers. When stories are enriched with predictive analytics, AI, and personalized content, they transcend into experiences that not only narrate but also adapt to the listener's own story. Such dynamic storytelling is the future of digital engagement, one that promises to keep the conversation between brands and consumers vibrantly alive.

In conclusion, the art of storytelling in digital campaigns is not merely about drafting an engaging narrative. It is about spellbinding an audience through relatable emotional journeys, staying true to a brand's essence while evolving with technological advancements. It is about the meticulous crafting of stories that are simple yet profound, consistent yet adaptable within the fabric of the digital mosaic. Mastery over this art form can turn browsers into buyers, customers into champions, and products into legacies.

As digital marketers, it is our charge to harness this ancient craft, wield it with ingenuity, and unfold stories that not only sell but also dignify the very essence of what it means to connect in this digital age. The written word is your wand; brand narratives are your spells. Cast them wisely, and watch your digital alchemy turn your campaigns into gold.

Chapter 4:
Visual Impact: Leveraging Images and Video

Mastering the art of written content positions you at the threshold of compelling digital communication, yet it's in the dynamic realm of visual storytelling where engagement often skyrockets. In Chapter 4, "Visual Impact: Leveraging Images and Video," we delve into the strategy of shaping perceptions and fostering connections through the power of visual media. The potent blend of images and videos is not merely a tactic but a bridge to the soul of your audience. The human brain processes visuals tens of thousands of times faster than text, which means every image or video you share can serve as a sophisticated missile in the attention economy, striking quickly and memorably. Whether it's an infographic that distills complex data into an impactful narrative or a video that weaves persuasive elements into its storytelling arc, your visual content must resonate, inspire, and, ultimately, convert. As we unpack the elements of visual persuasion, you'll learn to create content that not only captures attention but also holds it, turning viewers into advocates and customers into long-term partners. By harnessing the silent eloquence of visuals, your digital marketing strategy will acquire an indomitable force, standing out in an overcrowded digital landscape.

The Psychology Behind Visual Persuasion

In an age where screens are gateways to digital realms, a single image can turn the tides of consumer decision-making. As we delve into the psychology behind visual persuasion, it's crucial to understand how and why visuals can deeply influence online behavior, steering users towards particular actions and choices. This potent capability isn't just about aesthetics; it's steeped in our cognitive functions and emotional responses.

The human brain processes visuals *60,000 times faster* than text. That means the moment an image flashes before our eyes, we've already started to form an opinion or feeling towards it. This rapid processing allows images and videos to communicate complex messages succinctly, bypassing the verbal centers of the brain and directly connecting with our emotional cores.

Color psychology, a significant player in visual communication, taps into the subconscious associations humans have with certain hues. Warm colors can provoke excitement and urgency, while cool tones might evoke calmness and trust. Implementing a strategic color palette in your visuals isn't just about standing out; it's about conveying the right emotional message to your audience.

Composition and framing are equally influential. The way elements are arranged within an image can guide the viewer's eye seamlessly or create intentional tension. The rule of thirds, leading lines, and symmetry are more than photographic jargon; they are tools for persuasion, subtly directing attention to the most critical areas of your visual content.

Motion, be it through video or animation, garners an inherently high engagement. Video marketing, thus, becomes a powerhouse of persuasion. Motion catches the eye, and the dynamic unfolding of a narrative within a video can captivate an audience, take them on a journey, and prompt them to action more effectively than static images.

However, the persuasive power of video isn't just due to motion. It's the ability to merge visuals with sound and storytelling that renders it so compelling. A well-crafted video can elicit a range of emotions, driving empathy and forging a stronger emotional connection between the brand and the consumer.

Symbolism in visuals also holds persuasive weight. Icons and metaphors translate to universally recognized messages that span cultures and languages. They can resonate with a viewer's existing knowledge and beliefs, making concepts instantly relatable and persuasive without the need for lengthy explanations.

Images also benefit from the principle of social proof, wherein we look to others to determine correct behavior. For instance, a photograph depicting people enjoying a product can lead observers to believe the product is desirable and trusted by others, nudging them to adopt similar behaviors.

Persuasive visuals rely on the innate human attraction to stories. Through visual storytelling, brands can create relatable narratives that resonate with their audience's experiences and aspirations. An image can serve as a snapshot of a larger story, inviting the audience to imagine themselves within it, thus creating a powerful incentive for action.

Facial expressions and body language in visuals connect with the viewer on an empathic level. We are hardwired to respond to human faces, and visuals that include them can rapidly create a sense of connection and trust that might take paragraphs of text to establish.

But there's a subtler side to visual persuasion. It's in the spacing between elements, the typography of text, and even in what's *not* shown. Negative space, for example, can focus attention and create simplicity, conveying professionalism and confidence. In essence, the simplicity of design can suggest a product or service is equally straightforward and reliable.

Visual consistency is another psychological lever. When images across various digital channels maintain a cohesive style and theme, they strengthen brand recognition and trust. Consistency reinforces the identity of a brand, allowing it to become a familiar, reliable presence in the consumer's digital landscape.

Scarcity and exclusivity can also be conveyed visually. Limited-edition products, countdown clocks, and visuals that suggest a 'last chance' opportunity can create a sense of urgency, leveraging the fear of missing out (FOMO) to encourage quicker decision-making.

The psychology behind visual persuasion is deep-rooted in our evolutionary progress and adapted for the digital age. Leveraging this knowledge allows marketers to craft images and videos that not only attract attention but also speak to the core desires and emotions of their audience. It's about creating a visual handshake that is at once inviting and influential.

Therefore, as we look to harness the power of visuals, we must remember that they are more than just decorative elements. They are persuasive instruments that, when used with intention and understanding, can become the cornerstone of successful digital marketing strategies.

Video Marketing: The Persuasion Powerhouse

As we navigate through the intricate tapestry of digital marketing, a stellar transformation is evident. Video has emerged not just as a medium of expression, but as a persuasion powerhouse that commands attention and fosters deep, emotional connections with audiences. In a landscape where compelling narratives and dynamic visuals reign supreme, leveraging the nuances of video marketing is imperative for any brand looking to assert its influence and drive meaningful engagement.

The core of video marketing's efficacy stems from its unparalleled ability to synthesize storytelling and imagery. By tapping into this medium, brands breathe life into their messages, translating complex ideas into digestible, relatable content. Imagine the gripping allure of a well-crafted video; it showcases not only a product but weaves a narrative that viewers can picture themselves in. It's an immersive experience that appeals to the sensors and the imagination, leaving an enduring impression that static images and text simply can't match.

Understanding the psychological underpinnings of why video is so persuasive is essential. Humans are hardwired to respond to movement and faces. These elements, inherent to video, trigger emotional responses and make the content feel more personal and trustworthy. This visceral connection can be leveraged to guide audiences through a nuanced persuasion journey – from awareness and interest to desire and action.

Diving deeper, let's explore the facets of why video content is a must-have in your digital marketing arsenal. A well-executed video can give your brand a voice, an ethos, and a presence that resonates deeply with viewers. It is not solely about the product or service anymore; it's about fostering a brand image that aligns with the values and aspirations of your audience, subsequently nurturing brand loyalty and advocacy.

To effectively harness the power of video marketing, keep content engaging and accessible. Audiences are inundated with content, so brevity and clarity will ensure that your message stands out. Embrace the art of concise storytelling and prioritize quality over quantity. Video content should captivate within the first few seconds; this is your window to grab attention before viewers scroll away.

Remember to tailor your video strategy to your brand's unique value proposition and identity. It's not about mimicking the strategies of competitors, but rather, about carving out your own space within the visual ecosystem. What message does your brand seek to communicate, and how can video serve as the most potent medium to convey it?

While high production values can yield stunning results, do not be deterred by budget constraints. Authenticity often trumps glossy production. Users can connect more to a video that feels genuine and personal. Short, impromptu clips that offer a behind-the-scenes look into your brand's world can sometimes eclipse a high-budget commercial in terms of engagement and persuasion.

Video also serves as an outstanding platform for demonstrating the practicality and efficacy of products or services. If a picture is worth a thousand words, then a video is surely worth millions. Through demonstrations, testimonials, and in-depth explorations, potential customers can be transported beyond mere features, to a rich landscape of benefits and real-world applications.

Let's not overlook the analytic aspects of video marketing. With advanced tracking metrics, you can glean insights into how viewers engage with your content. Learning where they pause, rewind, or drop off provides invaluable feedback to refine your video content strategy continually.

Incorporate a strong call-to-action in your videos as it serves as the catalyst for the viewer's next step. Whether it's subscribing to a newsletter, visiting a website, or making a purchase, your video should guide them unequivocally to this point of conversion with clear and compelling prompts.

Integrating video content into all facets of your digital marketing strategy amplifies its influence. From social media snippets to comprehensive product walkthroughs on your website, multichannel dissemination ensures that your video content reaches the widest possible audience. Each platform offers unique opportunities for engagement and interaction, thus crafting a cohesive experience across the board is crucial.

Optimization for mobile viewing is no longer optional; it's outright essential. With the majority of video content being consumed on mobile devices, ensure that your videos are responsive, load quickly, and are compatible across various devices and screen sizes.

SEO considerations should not be neglected when it comes to video content. Using relevant keywords in your titles and descriptions, tagging accurately, and hosting your video content on platforms favored by search engines can greatly enhance your visibility and discoverability online. This approach will complement your SEO efforts and drive organic traffic to your content.

Lastly, always be willing to innovate and adapt. The digital landscape is in constant flux, with new trends and technologies emerging regularly. Embrace emerging formats like live streaming or 360-degree videos to stay ahead of the curve and keep your audience engaged and excited for what's next from your brand.

Video marketing, indeed, is the persuasion powerhouse we can't afford to ignore. It propels brands beyond the confines of traditional marketing into a realm where connection, engagement, and influence pave the way for unprecedented success. Harness this medium with creativity, intention, and strategic foresight, and you'll witness the compelling impact it can have on your digital persuasion strategy.

Infographics and Memes: Virality and Shareability

In the realm of digital marketing, visual content is king. With the saturation of textual information on the internet, infographics and memes have emerged as persuasive tools that break through the clutter and capture the audience's attention. The power of an infographic lies in its ability to distill complex data into a digestible and visually appealing format. Moreover, memes captivate through humor and relatability, often becoming cultural touchstones that spread like wildfire across the web.

Let's uncover the anatomy of virality within infographics. A well-crafted infographic is more than just an image; it's a storytelling device that leads the viewer's eye on a journey from point A to point B. The most effective infographics use a combination of compelling visuals and concise text to articulate a concept or data set quickly and clearly. They often leverage design principles such as color theory and typography to highlight key points and maintain viewer engagement.

Infographics encourage sharing because they offer value—whether in the form of knowledge, insight, or a solution to a problem. In fact, studies have shown that content with relevant images gets 94% more views than content without. This shareability factor is a goldmine for digital marketers looking to boost their brand's presence and reach a larger audience organically without a significant ad spend.

Memes, on the other hand, tap into the pulse of popular culture and human emotions. They are the epitome of simplicity, often consisting of a recognizable image coupled with a witty caption. Despite their simplicity, memes can be incredibly nuanced, reflecting current events, trends, and the collective mood of the internet community. Memes essentially become the language of the digital age, a way for people to communicate and connect over shared experiences.

But what makes infographics and memes so shareable? It can be attributed to their innate ability to elicit an emotional response, whether it's surprise, joy, or even indignation. When content triggers an emotion, it increases the likelihood that a person will pass it on; it's the concept of emotional contagion. A viewer is not just sharing an image; they're sharing a feeling, an idea, or an identity.

Another factor contributing to the virality of infographics and memes is their ease of consumption. In a fast-paced digital environment where attention spans are short, these visual forms can be processed 60,000 times faster than text. This immediacy not only makes them more accessible but also increases the chance that they will be spread across various platforms, reaching diverse audiences.

Marketers looking to capitalize on the viral potential of infographics and memes should focus on adaptability. The content must be easily adjustable to fit multiple platforms without losing its impact. Whether it's a static image on Instagram, a GIF on Twitter, or a snippet in a YouTube video, the core message should remain impactful and comprehensible.

Brand alignment is also a critical consideration. While memes in particular are notorious for their edgy humor, it's important that the content reflects the brand's values and messages without crossing any lines that could alienate the audience. Consistency in branding and messaging reinforces recognition and strengthens the connection with the audience.

Responsive interactivity with trending topics can be a game-changer. Infographics and memes that respond to real-time events or trending conversations can enjoy a surge in shares as they ride the wave of public interest. Nevertheless, marketers must exhibit nimbleness and sensitivity to ensure that their content is appropriate and adds meaningful discourse to the conversation.

Searchability is another aspect that shouldn't be overlooked. The textual context that accompanies infographics and memes can be optimized with keywords to enhance their discoverability through search engines—a process that can organically increase the visibility of the content beyond the immediate sphere of social media.

To fully utilize the potential of infographics and memes, digital marketers should also focus on syndication strategies. Partnering with influencers, leveraging email newsletters, and contributing to online communities can help spread visual content to new, larger, and more engaged audiences.

Analytics plays a crucial role in understanding what resonates with the audience. Testing different styles and themes of infographics and memes can provide valuable insights into preferences and tendencies, allowing marketers to refine their approach for maximum impact and shareability.

Lastly, let's not forget about the longevity of these visual assets. While memes may be more ephemeral due to their reliance on the zeitgeist, well-constructed infographics can continue to drive traffic and engagement long after their initial publication. They can be repurposed as educational tools, integrated into presentations, and used to build a more comprehensive digital asset library that continues to showcase the brand's expertise and value proposition over time.

The fusion of art and data represented in infographics and the social commentary encapsulated in memes hold immense power in the current marketing landscape. They aren't just accessories to text-based content; they are standalone pillars that can propel a marketing strategy forward through their virality and shareability. Harnessing this power demands creativity, alignment with the brand's voice, and a finger on the pulse of what captures the digital audience's attention.

Infographics and memes have rewritten the rules of engagement, offering an accelerated path to brand visibility and audience connection. By crafting content that can be quickly understood, instantly felt, and easily shared, digital marketers and brands can make an indelible imprint in the minds of their audience—one impactful image at a time.

Chapter 5:
Social Media Dynamics

As we dive into the fabric of social media, we recognize it as the ever-evolving tapestry of human connection and influence. In the world where these platforms reign, grasping the unique language and behavior on each is crucial. Facebook's landscape thrives on community and trust, requiring a nuanced approach that fosters dialogue and connection. Instagram, with its visual feast, demands a carefully curated aesthetic, instantly signalling value through images that speak louder than words. LinkedIn operates on a different vibration, one of professionalism and network-building that can unlock doors to opportunities when navigated with savvy. It's about much more than posting and praying—It's crafting a strategy that resonates on a visceral level, where every like, share, and comment is a testimony to the digital alchemy at work. And with the precision of social media advertising, the message is no longer a shout into the void but a targeted whisper into the right ears, leveraging algorithms and insights to sway hearts and minds with striking accuracy. This chapter will not just skim the surface but delve deep into the mechanics of these platforms to amplify your digital essence, sculpting a presence that not only exists but powerfully persuades in this social media driven realm.

Navigating Different Social Platforms

In the spirited realm of social media, mastering the nuances of each platform heralds the triumph of a persuasive digital presence. As a marketer, entrepreneur, or business maverick, recognizing that each social landscape demands its unique tactic is non-negotiable; a one-size-fits-all approach is a relic best left untouched. The savvy navigator knows that Twitter's brevity and speed can amplify a concise message, while Pinterest's visual playground beckons an entirely different strategy that appeals to the dreamers and planners. To weave persuasion through the fibers of these varied tapestries, it's vital to adapt your voice to resonate with the distinct audience each platform harbors, from the professional corridors of LinkedIn to the vibrant communities of TikTok. Dive into the ecosystem of each domain with an appetite for learning and a flexibility that allows you to tailor content that not only engages but also converts, always staying two steps ahead in the digital ballet of platform-specific nuances.

Facebook: Building Community and Trust

The journey through the landscape of digital persuasion brings us to the venerable giant, Facebook, a platform where community and trust are the linchpins of a successful presence. With billions of users, Facebook holds an unparalleled position in the digital realm. The key to leveraging this platform is not in simply broadcasting messages but in fostering a sense of community and cultivating trust among your audience.

Building community on Facebook begins with understanding your audience. Who are they? What are their interests, fears, and desires? When you pinpoint your audience's core characteristics, you can start meaningful conversations and develop content that resonates. A community thrives on engagement. Encouraging your audience to interact not only with you but also with each other creates a vibrant ecosystem around your brand.

Creating a Facebook group adjacent to your business page opens up a space for deeper engagement. Consider these groups as the meeting rooms where your customers gather to discuss your products, share experiences, and offer feedback. By actively participating and moderating these groups, you create a nurturing environment that represents a safe space for discussion, driving up trust and loyalty.

Trust on Facebook is not just built through direct interaction; content plays a vital role as well. Sharing valuable content that solves problems or enlightens your audience positions your brand as a trustworthy source. Utilize Facebook's various content formats like posts, images, and videos to provide a rich and diverse content experience that keeps your audience informed and engaged.

Another aspect worth integrating is storytelling. Your brand's narrative should weave through every piece of content you share, resonating with the emotive strings of your audience's hearts. Real stories about challenges, triumphs, and lessons learned showcase your brand's authenticity and create deeper connections.

Consistency is critical. A consistent voice and posting schedule provide a sense of reliability. Your community should know when to expect new content from you—like a familiar rhythm that becomes part of their online experience. Consistency also extends to the tone and quality of your interactions. Polite, prompt, and positive engagements reinforce a trustworthy brand image.

Facebook's algorithm favors content that generates conversation and meaningful interaction. As a digital marketer, you must craft content that not only attracts attention but also prompts dialogue. Questions, polls, and calls to action are effective tools that can increase engagement and, consequently, expand organic reach.

Customer feedback on Facebook is a double-edged sword, yet it's an essential tool for building trust. Addressing complaints and criticism quickly and empathetically turns negative experiences into opportunities for public demonstration of your brand's commitment to customer satisfaction. Equally important is celebrating positive feedback, which reinforces the positive aspects of your brand and encourages more of the same.

Privacy and transparency on Facebook are pivotal in establishing trust. With digital privacy concerns at an all-time high, being upfront about how you collect and use data reassures your community that you value and protect their personal information. This transparency creates a bedrock of trust that supports all your persuasive efforts on the platform.

Collaborations and partnerships can enhance community building on Facebook. Pairing up with complementary brands or influencers who share your values can introduce your brand to new audiences. These strategic partnerships should harmonize with your community's interests, providing an integrative approach to expanding your reach while maintaining coherence within your brand's ecosystem.

Monitoring and analytics are crucial for understanding the dynamics of your Facebook community. Pay close attention to what types of content generate the most engagement, what times your audience is most active, and how they interact with your brand across different posts. Use this data to refine your strategy, ensuring you're always aligning with your community's preferences and behaviors.

The role of Facebook Advertising should not be overlooked. It's a powerful tool for reaching a broader audience and drawing them into your community. However, the goal should always be to transition from paid interactions to organic ones over time. Ads should be thought of as conversation starters, leading to authentic engagements that grow the community.

The principle of social proof is magnified on Facebook. When people see others interacting positively with your brand, it reinforces trust and confidence. Showcase customer testimonials, user-generated content, and success stories to leverage this powerful form of persuasion. Social proof acts as a beacon, drawing others to your community and amplifying the persuasive power of your brand.

A proactive approach to conflict resolution is necessary to maintain trust within the community. Misunderstandings will arise, and when they do, how you handle them can make or break your brand image. Be timely, gracious, and solution-focused when conflicts surface. This demonstrates your commitment to the well-being of your community and upholds the trust you've worked hard to establish.

In the transformative space of Facebook, building community and trust requires a multifaceted approach—rooted in authenticity and sustained by consistent, respectful engagement. It's not merely about having a presence but about nurturing a living, breathing community that believes in your brand and its promise. So, dive into creating a Facebook community where trust becomes the currency, and watch as the power of persuasion unfolds through the strength of the connections you've fortified.

Instagram: A Picture's Worth a Thousand Words

In an age where our attention is a prized commodity, Instagram has risen as a visual powerhouse in the digital marketing arsenal. This platform, at its core, allows for storytelling through imagery, metamorphosing simple snapshots into powerful narratives. Let's unwrap the kinetic energy contained within a single image and how, as marketers, we can harness this power to not only capture attention but also to enchant and persuade an audience.

Instagram utilizes visuals to cast a spell on viewers, and marketers can create an entire brand story in a single frame. Its mosaic feed becomes a tapestry, weaving together moments that, collectively, portray the ethos of your brand. Understanding that each picture contributes to the larger narrative is essential. Strategically placing each post is akin to choosing the next piece in a puzzle that, when completed, will showcase a larger picture that's compelling and rich with purpose.

Engagement on Instagram is king. Yet it's not just about the number of likes or comments; it's about the quality of interactions. Persuasion begins the moment a user feels connected to the content. Crafting images that resonate personally with viewers, that speak to their aspirations, pain points, and joys, requires a keen understanding of not just what is visually appealing, but also what is emotionally stirring.

Evoke emotion using colors, textures, and subjects that touch upon the universal human experience. Every hue and tone carries its own psychological weight, serving to draw viewers into a desired state of mind. A well-thought-out color scheme can convey a mood without saying a word, whether it's the tranquility of soft blues or the energetic pop of vibrant oranges.

Always keep in mind the power of composition in your visuals. The relationship between objects within an image can tell a story of connection or disparity. Leading lines draw the eye towards a focal point, while the use of space can highlight the prominence of a subject or concept. By masterfully crafting each post's composition, you invite your audience to enter into a narrative crafted just for them.

Hashtags and captions can't be overlooked; they act as a bridge between visual content and verbal messaging. They provide context and can guide the viewer to a deeper understanding of the image. A cleverly written caption can reinforce the persuasion begun by the visual, making the combination a potent tool for influencing and engaging your audience. The right hashtag, meanwhile, extends the reach of your message to the widest relevant audience.

User-generated content on Instagram is a goldmine for marketers. It's social proof crystallized. By showcasing how others use and enjoy your product or service, you create an infectious cycle of sharing and engagement. This not only bolsters your brand's credibility but also immerses potential customers in a community that's already enjoying what you have to offer.

The feature set of Instagram, including Stories, Reels, IGTV, and live videos, affords numerous avenues for creativity and engagement. Stories, fleeting by design, offer an ephemeral canvas for behind-the-scenes peeks, limited-time offers, or spontaneous bursts of brand personality. Reels and IGTV dive into longer forms of content that can capture intricate narratives or detailed showcases of products.

Authenticity shines bright on Instagram. Today's savvy consumers can sniff out disingenuous content from a mile away. Authentic storytelling that aligns with your brand values can break down barriers and build trust. This emotional investment from your viewers can turn followers into brand advocates, amplifying your message across their own networks.

Consistency in posting is more than a mere strategy; it's a promise of reliability to your audience. A regular posting schedule keeps your brand top-of-mind and provides a stable rhythm of content that followers can anticipate and look forward to. However, this doesn't mean sacrificing quality for quantity. Balancing regular updates with high-quality content is a tightrope walk that pays dividends in audience loyalty.

Influencer partnerships on Instagram can bolster the impact of your brand's visual storytelling. Tap into influencers whose audiences align with your target demographic. Their endorsement can serve as a powerful form of social proof, persuading their followers to view your products with a familiar trust.

Interactive elements within the platform, such as polls, quizzes, and question stickers in Stories, draw the audience into a dialogue. They are not just passive viewers but active participants in your marketing journey. These tools can provide valuable insights into your audience's preferences and encourage a sense of ownership in your brand's direction.

Creating exclusivity through limited-time offers or insider information can leverage the principle of scarcity. When followers believe they're getting access to something unique and time-sensitive, the desire to act is heightened. Use stories and temporary posts to highlight these offers, creating a compelling reason for immediate engagement.

The integration of commerce features on Instagram has created a seamless pathway from persuasion to purchase. Tagged products, shopping pages, and direct checkout options simplify the conversion process. By minimizing barriers to purchase, your Instagram feed becomes not just a gallery, but a storefront, turning casual browsers into buyers almost effortlessly.

Always remember, agility is vital. The digital landscape is always shifting, and Instagram is no exception. Stay abreast of current trends, features, and algorithm changes to keep your strategy as sharp as your imagery. By using Instagram as a multi-faceted tool designed for visual persuasion, you'll reach into the hearts and minds of your audience, earning their attention and motivating their actions. A picture on Instagram can indeed be worth a thousand words, but more importantly, it can be worth countless connections.

LinkedIn: Networking and Persuasion Among Professionals

LinkedIn stands apart in the social media landscape as a powerhouse for professional networking and persuasion. It's where connections are not merely about social interactions, but about building bridges that lead to fruitful professional relationships and business opportunities. As digital marketers, it's imperative to understand the nuances of communicating on this platform, where the language of business mingles with the subtle art of persuasion.

Imagine LinkedIn as a vast sea of professionals—each potentially a key influencer in their respective fields. It's a place where your profile is your digital handshake, and every post or message must convey not just information, but also credibility and value. To harness the platform's full potential, it's essential to construct a strategic approach, starting with your professional identity.

Your profile on LinkedIn acts as your digital ambassador. It's critical to ensure that it reflects authority and expertise in your field. Every endorsement, recommendation, or skill listed can be a testament to your professional standing. To persuade, you must first establish a foundation of trust, and a well-crafted LinkedIn profile is the cornerstone of that trust.

Networking on LinkedIn isn't about amassing a random collection of contacts. It's about strategic relationship building. Identifying and connecting with the right individuals can grant you access to thought leaders and decision-makers. By engaging with their content thoughtfully, you can pave the way for meaningful interactions that may translate into opportunities.

Content creation on LinkedIn is another avenue where persuasion takes center stage. It's not just about what you say, but how you say it. Crafting articles, posts, and sharing insights that add genuine value can position you as a thought leader. This content is your opportunity to demonstrate expertise and convey your unique perspective to your network.

Persuasion on LinkedIn also comes in the form of recommendations and endorsements. These social proofs are powerful because they come from peers and colleagues who can vouch for your competencies. Garnering such testimonials requires not just skill but also the generosity of giving recommendations to others in a sincere and meaningful way, which often leads to reciprocation.

Joining and participating in relevant LinkedIn groups can significantly expand your network and influence. These communities allow you to demonstrate your knowledge and participate in conversations that matter to your industry. By providing insightful answers and starting discussions, you can persuade group members of your expertise and value to the community.

LinkedIn Ads offer a targeted approach to persuasion. With its robust targeting capabilities, you can deliver content and messages directly to the professionals most likely to be influenced by your products or services. The key lies in crafting compelling ad copy and using strong calls to action that resonate with the specific needs and interests of your target audience.

As a platform rich with data, LinkedIn provides valuable insights that can refine your persuasion strategy. By understanding who views your profile and content, you can tailor your messaging to more closely align with the interests of your audience. Analyzing these metrics allows for continuous optimization of your approach.

Personalized messaging on LinkedIn can be especially persuasive. Whether reaching out to a new connection or following up with a lead, personalized messages can significantly increase your chances of receiving a favorable response. People appreciate feeling recognized as individuals, rather than just another contact in a list.

Automation tools, while useful in managing LinkedIn activity, should be used sparingly. Authenticity in your interactions is key to convincing others of your sincerity. Automated messages may save time, but nothing beats a personalized touch when it comes to building relationships that matter.

LinkedIn's unique feature of endorsements allows professionals to validate each other's skills. However, to influence effectively through endorsements, it's crucial to first make meaningful contributions to your network. Skills and endorsements become vastly more persuasive when they reflect real professional appreciation.

Video content is increasingly gaining traction on LinkedIn. Videos offer a dynamic way to express your brand's story and value proposition. Creating compelling video content that addresses the pain points of your network can be a powerful tool in garnering attention and swaying opinion in your favor.

Thought leadership on LinkedIn is not about selling; it's about educating and informing. By sharing your insights and knowledge, you build a following of professionals who trust and respect your views. This trust creates a foundation upon which persuasion can occur naturally and more effectively.

Finally, the principle of reciprocity plays a significant role in LinkedIn networking. By supporting others—whether through sharing their content or offering help and advice—you create a culture of mutual assistance. This culture fosters an environment where others are more inclined to support and be persuaded by you in return.

Mastering networking and persuasion on LinkedIn is an exercise in balance—balancing self-promotion with altruism, automation with personalization, and content creation with engagement. When harmonized skillfully, these elements come together to create a powerful platform for professional growth and influence. Embrace

LinkedIn as the sophisticated tool it is, and it can become a game-changer for your digital marketing aspirations.

Social Media Advertising: Targeted Persuasion

With an understanding of different social platforms established, it's imperative we delve into the nuanced realm of social media advertising and its capacity for targeted persuasion. This medium has transformed brand-consumer interactions, offering an unparalleled opportunity for businesses to communicate with their audience on a deeply personalized level.

Social media platforms have become the modern-day marketplace, not merely for products, but for ideas, narratives, and influences. In this intricate dance of communication, targeted ads play a crucial role; they serve as the bridge connecting a brand's vision to the consumer's desires. At its core, targeted persuasion is about understanding the multi-faceted profiles of your audience and presenting them with content that resonates powerfully.

To leverage such targeted persuasion, we must begin with granular audience segmentation. The more detailed your audience personas, the more effectively you can tailor your messaging. Data points that inform these personas stem from demographic information, psychographic profiling, and consumer behaviors—all of which social media channels can provide in abundance.

Upon identifying your target audience, crafting a tailored message becomes key. This isn't merely about selling a product or service; it's about creating a message that aligns with the worldview of your audience. By validating their beliefs, you're not just attracting attention, you're earning trust.

The strategy multiplies in complexity when considering the creative elements of your ads. Visual cues, emotional triggers, and memorable content collectively foster a relationship between your brand and the customer. Aligning these creative elements with the psychographic profile of your target audience can increase the potential impact of your advertising exponentially.

Part of targeted persuasion is about timing. The precision with which you can now target based on not just who your audience is, but where they are in their consumer journey, can define the success of a campaign. This involves delivering the right message at the right time, a concept often referred to as 'moment marketing'.

Social media platforms offer advertising tools that can match your content with users based on their recent activity, life events, and even sentiment. Utilizing these tools creates an advertising experience that feels less like a broad broadcast and more like a conversation.

Engagement metrics also play a vital role. They offer insights into what captures your audience's attention, compels action, and generates emotional resonance. This feedback loop should inform ad optimizations, enabling a continuously improving campaign performance. A well-engaged audience is also more likely to become brand ambassadors, further amplifying your message.

Retargeting strategies add another layer to targeted persuasion. By re-engaging individuals who have shown interest in your brand, either by visiting your website or interacting with previous content, you remain top-of-mind. This is where the subtleties of frequency and messaging play a critical role; retargeting should feel like a natural continuation of the user's engagement with your brand.

Moreover, the integration of social proof through testimonials, user-generated content, and social sharing can scale the effectiveness of your ads. It's the digital equivalent of word-of-mouth marketing, and it can greatly amplify the credibility and appeal of your offerings. People trust people, and when ads feature real-world validation, the persuasive power skyrockets.

Along with social proof, collaborations with influencers can be a game-changer. When a trusted personality advocates for your brand within the context of their regular content, the message is not perceived as an ad but as an endorsement from a credible source. This subtle form of persuasion melds seamlessly into the user's social media experience.

However, in a world brimming with content competition, creativity is the linchpin of visibility. Out-of-the-box concepts and campaigns that challenge norms or touch on the zeitgeist can experience virality. Creativity in advertising, when executed with an understanding of the target audience, can lead to substantial persuasion through shared cultural moments.

It's important to never lose sight of the fact that targeted persuasion should not equate to manipulation. The ethics of your advertising approach must align with transparent and honest communication. When persuasion through social media advertising upholds integrity, it not only captures attention but nurtures lasting relationships.

Lastly, no advertising effort is set in stone. Test, measure, and refine should become your mantra. Social media platforms provide a plethora of analytic tools that allow you to track the performance of your ads in real-time. Use the data to discern not just what worked, but why it worked, providing you the insights to hone your strategy to razor-sharp precision.

In conclusion, leveraging targeted persuasion in social media advertising demands a sophisticated blend of audience understanding, creative messaging, strategic timing, ethical practice, and continuous refinement. By mastering these aspects, you elevate your brand from mere presence to persuasive power on social media—a vital shift in the digital age where visibility must be matched by influence.

Chapter 6:
SEO and SEM: Being Found Online

In the continuously evolving theater of digital marketing, visibility is not just about being seen; it's about being found with intention and relevance. As we delve into Chapter 6, we'll navigate the intricate web of search engine optimization (SEO) and search engine marketing (SEM), teaching you to harness the twin tools that ensure your brand stands out in the ocean of online content. This isn't just about attracting eyeballs; it's about drawing in the right audience with surgical precision through the art of persuasion search engines understand. Here, you'll learn to conduct keyword research with the finesse of a linguist, decoding the intent behind every search and aligning it with your offerings. We'll guide you through the intricacies of crafting meta descriptions and titles that aren't just a collection of keywords, but persuasive pitches that compel clicks. By mastering SEO and SEM, you're not just climbing the ranks of search results; you're building bridges of relevance between your brand and the audience who are already seeking solutions you provide. It's not enough to be part of the digital conversation; with the strategies in this chapter, you'll be leading it, driving traffic, and unlocking the online potential of your brand.

The Art of Persuading Search Engines

Entering the arena of search engines is akin to stepping into a vast ocean where countless streams of data flow and converge. To navigate these waters effectively, one must not only understand the tides but also speak the language of the ocean itself. The art of persuading search engines begins with communicating in the lexicon of relevance, authority, and trust.

Persuasion, in digital terms, is about making your online presence compelling to not just human visitors but also to the algorithms that dictate visibility. Search Engine Optimization (SEO) and Search Engine Marketing (SEM) are pillars that support the structure of online discoverability. It's within this framework that businesses can exhibit their mastery over the art of digital persuasion.

How does one weave the language of SEO and SEM into their online tapestry? Start by understanding that search engines are on a relentless quest to satisfy user queries with the highest quality and most relevant content. Every update to their algorithms fine-tunes their ability to discern and elevate such content. Your mission should be to signal to these algorithms that your site not only contains the answers to these queries but that it does so in a manner that is accessible, informative, and authoritative.

Keywords form the foundation of this communication. They are the succinct summary of query intentions, a distillation of need into a few pivotal words. But keywords alone are like single notes without a melody; they need context and composition to truly resonate. Therefore, comprehensive keyword research that dives deep into user intent is paramount. The strategic placement of these terms, with an ear for natural language and an eye for user experience, creates a harmony search engines can appreciate.

SEO is not just about keywords though; it's about crafting a narrative that encompasses them. Compelling content that serves the user's need and captures their interest signals to search engines that your page is a valuable resource. This content must be well-structured, incorporating headers and subheaders that guide both readers and search engine crawlers through the logical progression of ideas.

In the background, a robust technical SEO strategy ensures that your site is navigable by the web's many explorers: the search engine bots. A site's architecture, its loading speed, its responsiveness to different devices, and its inclusivity through accessible design—all these factors contribute to the perceived authority of your digital domain.

You persuade search engines through consistency as well. Like a reliable friend, your site must offer stability in quality and factual accuracy. Inconsistent information or broken links damage credibility. The careful management of your online presence, including attentive updates and maintenance, builds a reputation of reliability with search engines much as it does with human visitors.

Don't overlook the persuasive power of connections. In the vast web of digital information, links are like handshakes, introducing and vouching for participants. A robust backlink profile from reputable, well-regarded sites is a vote of confidence that search algorithms value highly. It's a testimony of your site's worth within the wider digital community.

Moving on to SEM, the art of persuasion takes a more direct route. Paid search advertising is the equivalent of having a bright billboard along the information superhighway. These targeted ads require a keen sense of timing and understanding of consumer behavior to ensure that they appear when and where potential customers are most likely to be swayed by them. Craft your ad copy with a precision that mirrors your best content—the message should be clear, value-driven, and action-oriented.

Analytics serve as your compass in this landscape. Regular analysis of your data tells you not just where you've been, but also where you should go. Patterns emerge that point to successful strategies as well as areas in need of improvement. Adjust and fine-tune your efforts based on solid, analytical reasoning rather than intuition alone.

The art of persuasion when dealing with search engines requires a dynamic approach, adapting as the algorithms evolve. Search engines value user experience above all, and as search behaviors change, so too must your tactics. Stay informed of the latest trends and algorithm updates to ensure that your strategies remain effective.

Technical aspects aside, remember that at its heart, persuading search engines is about serving the searcher. Fulfill their needs in a way that is both genuine and helpful, and the algorithms will take notice. There is no greater persuasion technique than demonstrating value; do so consistently, and your place within the search engine rankings will reflect that.

Ultimately, the art of persuading search engines is one of balancing human-centered content with search-centric technical nuances. It requires a constant learning mindset, an openness to innovation, and a commitment to quality. The rewards for mastering this craft are clear—a prominent presence in an ever-growing digital world where being found is paramount to success.

As you continue to refine your approach, weave these insights into the very fabric of your digital marketing efforts. With each step, you're not just persuading search engines; you're building bridges to the very individuals in search of the solutions you offer. That's the heart of digital marketing, the soul of your online existence—connecting people with the answers they seek, one search at a time.

So let the art of persuasion be your guiding light in an ever-changing digital landscape. It's not just about climbing to the top; it's about staying there, relevant and resonant in the chorus of voices vying for attention. Move forward with purpose, understanding that the true measure of your success is in the connections you create, the needs you meet, and the value you bring to the digital table.

Keyword Research: Understanding User Intent

When it comes to being found online, understanding the intentions behind a user's search query is not just a clever tactic, it's the fulcrum upon which the lever of SEO swings. Keyword research morphs from a mere task into an odyssey of comprehending the psyche of your potential customer. What are they truly seeking when they type that phrase into the search bar? This understanding is the cornerstone of unlocking the relevance of your content in the vast digital expanse.

Consider the landscape of the internet as a bustling marketplace, where every stall vies for the patron's attention. But to capture that attention, you must first discern why they're strolling through the lanes of this virtual bazaar. Is it to buy, to learn, or merely to browse? Each purpose entails a different approach in your digital conversation.

The age-old marketing wisdom tells us that people don't want quarter-inch drills; they want quarter-inch holes. Apply this adage to your keyword strategy. Engage with the why behind the search, not just the what. Start by classifying intent into buckets: informational, navigational, transactional, and commercial. Each bucket demands different content, a different voice, and a different strategy.

Informational searches indicate curiosity and a hunger for knowledge. These users might not be poised to purchase but nurturing them with rich educational content could gently usher them down the sales funnel. Crafting content with these users in mind involves answering questions, offering insights, and becoming a beacon of information they come to rely on.

Navigational queries are a sign that your brand has penetrated the psyche of your audience. They seek you out amidst the clamor, a testament to your branding efforts. In these instances, the path has to be clear and direct, leading them swiftly to the information or page they desire.

Where the rubber meets the road is in the transactional searches. Here the user's intent is clear – they have their wallets out, ready to engage in commerce. For the savvy marketer, the keywords in this category are gold dust. Creating content with transactional intent means optimizing for conversions with persuasive calls-to-action and clear value propositions.

Commercial intent treads the line between informational and transactional queries. Users are potential buyers, but perhaps they need that final nudge - a comparison, a review, a demonstration of value. Your content here plays the role of a trusted advisor, guiding them towards making an informed choice.

Keyword research tools are invaluable in this mission. They help reveal not just popular search terms, but the frequency, competition, and sometimes even the nuances of language users employ. Armed with this intelligence, you can tailor your content to mirror the language and meet the expectations of your potential customers.

Long-tail keywords are like the secret passageways of SEO. These phrases, longer and more specific, might attract fewer searches, but they're brimming with intent. It's like targeting the customer who knows exactly what they want, down to the last detail, and all you need to do is be there, ready to serve.

But keyword research isn't a one-off quest. It's an ongoing pursuit, a continuous dialogue where you listen, adapt, and refine. Search trends are as fickle as they are revealing, often shaped by cultural shifts, technological advancements, and seasonal changes. Staying abreast of these tides means maintaining relevance in a sea of change.

Aligning keyword research with your content strategy unleashes its full potential. It transforms semantics into sales, curiosity into conversions. Each piece of content becomes a carefully crafted message, targeted to address the specific needs, pain points, and desires of your audience.

Not to be overlooked, the context of a search query adds depth to your understanding of user intent. Integrating search context allows you to discern between a query made in haste for immediate need and one made leisurely, with time to browse and compare. Grasping this can fine-tune how you position your content.

Keyword research also forewarns you of the battles ahead. It's impractical to gun for supremacy in an arena dominated by juggernauts when a more niche battleground can lead to greater victories. Recognize where you can realistically rank and direct your efforts for the highest return on investment.

Your empathy as a marketer comes into play as you interpret the data. Behind every typed phrase, there's a living, breathing human being with a task at hand. Your role? To provide them with a seamless journey that not only answers their query but eases the effort they must expend to arrive at the solution.

As you wield the power of keyword research, remember that user intent is dynamic. It evolves in parallel with your audience's journey. Beginning with awareness and culminating in action, your task is to guide them through this passage, providing relevant content at every twist and turn.

The dance between SEO and the user's intent is intricate and intimate. Mastering this dance doesn't just put you on the leaderboard; it sets the stage for you to choreograph a narrative that resonates deeply with your audience and compels them to act. In the intricate art of being found online, the clarity of user intent not only illuminates the path for your audience but also paves your trajectory towards digital marketing mastery.

Crafting Persuasive Meta Descriptions and Titles

In the realm of digital discovery, the significance of well-crafted meta descriptions and titles can't be overstated. These seemingly small components are tangible threads in the vast web of SEO and SEM strategies that help your content stand out amidst a sea of data, capturing the attention of both search engines and searchers. Let's delve into the art of constructing these powerful snippets that can dramatically bolster your online visibility.

Meta titles serve as succinct beacons that signal the essence of your webpage's content. They're the first touchpoint of engagement with your audience, conveying relevance and intent. Practice restraint as you craft these titles; brevity paired with strong keywords creates a beacon that guides users to your digital doorstep. An effective title isn't just about pleasing algorithms, it's a delicate balance, harmonizing SEO needs with the expectation and intrigue of your target audience.

Algining with this, meta descriptions play the role of a persuasive concierge. While titles hook attention, descriptions invite users into the conversation, offering a clear, compelling reason to click through to your page. A meta description is your opportunity to provide context, tease content, and differentiate from competitors all within about 160 characters. This is your sales pitch, succinctly summarizing the value proposition held within the webpage.

Embrace clarity and specificity in your meta descriptions. Generic statements lack the allure necessary to draw users in. Instead, pinpoint what makes your content unique and craft a message that encapsulates that uniqueness. Whether it's an exclusive offer, a unique insight, or an answer to a burning question, your description should pack a persuasive punch.

Keywords are the connective tissue between user queries and your content. Weave these into your titles and descriptions strategically, mirroring the language your audience uses. Aligning your meta elements with user intent is pivotal, as it increases the relevance of your content to those searching for solutions or information you provide.

Yet, avoid the temptation to stuff these fields with keywords. Keyword stuffing can backfire, leading to penalties from search engines and turning off potential visitors. Your aim is not to game the system but to gracefully inform and lure the right audience with honesty and precision.

Creativity holds a seat at the table when drafting meta descriptions and titles. Users are inundated with options, and a dash of creativity can make your link the one they choose to explore. Posing questions, leveraging powerful adjectives, and infusing your brand's voice can transform a mundane meta into a compelling call-to-action.

Consistency amplifies trust in the eyes of your audience. Ensure your meta titles and descriptions align with the content on your pages. A disconnect between what's promised in the search result and what's delivered can erode credibility and increase bounce rates, signaling to search engines that your content may not be as relevant as it claims to be.

In the broader perspective of SEO and SEM, meta descriptions and titles are not stand-alone elements; they are part of a persuasive ecosystem that includes URL structure, content quality, and user experience. This interconnectedness means that as you refine your meta elements, you must also ensure that they are working harmoniously with other on-page and off-page SEO efforts.

A/B testing is an invaluable tool in honing your meta descriptions and titles. Experiment with different versions to see which resonates more with your audience. Through data-driven analysis, you can optimize these elements to achieve the highest click-through rates and engagement.

Remember, however, that search engine algorithms are constantly evolving. What works today may not hold the same influence tomorrow. Stay informed of the latest updates and adapt your strategies to maintain peak performance in your meta descriptions and titles as well as other aspects of SEO and SEM.

As mobile search continues to soar, remember that brevity and clarity become even more paramount. With less screen space to captivate users, every character must work harder to persuade. Craft your meta elements with a mobile-first approach, ensuring they're optimized for readability and impact on smaller devices.

Evergreen content presents a unique opportunity for meta descriptions and titles. By crafting ever-relevant meta elements that endure beyond the temporal flux, you ensure a lasting appeal that continually attracts organic traffic. Aim for timelessness in your message where appropriate, so that it stays fresh and relevant regardless of season or trend.

In conclusion, the thoughtful crafting of meta descriptions and titles is a refined skill that melds creativity with strategic insight. It's about understanding the psyche of your user, matching your message to their search-intent, and delivering it in a way that is both noticeable and appealing to search engine algorithms. Ignite curiosity and provide value in these small but mighty snippets, and watch as your digital presence amplifies and your pages become the chosen destination for your targeted visitors.

With the foundational knowledge provided in the previous chapters and a strategic approach to these meta elements, you're well on your way to conquering the digital landscape. The compass points of persuasion, clarity, and creativity will guide you in crafting meta descriptions and titles that not only resonate with your audience but also reward you with the traction and engagement your online content deserves.

Chapter 7:
Data-Driven Persuasion

In an era where intuition is enhanced by insights and anomalies are parsed by algorithms, 'Data-Driven Persuasion' forms the crux of evolving digital marketing strategies. Moving past the rudimentary grasp of audience demographics and psychographics, this chapter unveils how quantifying customer interactions paves the way for hyper-personalized campaigns that resonate with precision, capturing not just the eye, but the heart of the market. We delve into the intelligent utilization of analytics to tailor experiences that not only charm audiences but also compel action, all the while maintaining an unwavering focus on the return on investment. Innovative A/B testing methodologies are dissected, enabling a rigorous, scientific approach to optimizing every touchpoint in a user's journey. As we dissect the arsenal of data at our disposal, we learn to craft messages that feel serendipitously aligned with individual desires, achieving the ultimate persuasion tool: personalization. By the chapter's end, harnessing the power of data won't merely be a facet of digital marketing—it'll be second nature, a driving force behind decisions that propel brands to monumental success in an ever-competitive digital landscape.

Utilizing Analytics for a Persuasion Edge

In the dynamic sphere of digital marketing, understanding the nuances of your audience's engagements can be the tipping point between a successful campaign and one that fades into oblivian. Analytics stand as the navigational compass guiding marketers through the stormy seas of the internet, providing a quantifiable measure for the subtle art of persuasion.

To wield analytics as a tool for persuasion, it's not merely about dousing in the sea of data but about fishing out the relevant metrics that align with your persuasion goals. It begins with setting clear and actionable objectives. Do you wish to enhance your website's conversion rate, or are you focused on increasing customer engagement on your latest post? Define your battlefields because analytics is the strategy that will lead you to victory.

At the heart of analytics-driven persuasion is the ability to identify patterns within user behavior. By analyzing where visitors linger, what they click, and when they bounce, one can interpret the silent signals that indicate what entices or deters your audience. In this way, each click is like a compass point, guiding you to create more engaging and persuasive content.

Let's consider segmentation: categorizing your audience based on their behavior can reveal how different groups interact with your content. Leveraging this information means you can tailor your persuasive techniques accordingly. For instance, a cohort that frequently engages with tutorial videos on your site may resonate more with in-depth educational content, guiding your content creation in a valuable direction.

Conversion tracking is yet another facet of analytics that can sharpen your persuasive edge. By understanding what percentage of users take the desired action, you can identify which aspects of your strategy are your aces and which are your setbacks. It's like solving a puzzle; each conversion leads to a clearer picture of what content convinces your audience to take the leap.

The velocity of data collection through analytics is astonishing, enabling real-time adjustments to campaigns. You're not waiting for the curtain to fall before gauging the audience's applause. Instead, you're tweaking the performance as it's happening, ensuring that your message resonates in the immediate present.

Heatmaps represent another crucial analytical tool. By visually showcasing where users are clicking, hovering, or scrolling on your page, they illuminate the hotspots of user engagement. This is akin to reading the audience's body language, adjusting your gesture and tone to hold their undivided attention.

Time analytics also reveal when your audience is most active and susceptible to persuasion. Timing your messaging can be just as crucial as the message itself, much like a comedian mastering the pause before the punchline. Send that persuasive email just when your audience is primed to read it, and you'll see engagement soar.

Beyond individual campaigns, analytics can also enhance your overall website's persuasiveness. By analyzing user flows, you can smooth out the path of navigation on your site, gently guiding visitors from introduction to conversion with elegance and ease.

Customer feedback collected through analytics shouldn't be overlooked either. Reviews, ratings, and direct comments hold the keys to understanding your audience on a more personal level. This empathetic understanding becomes the bedrock upon which you craft more relatable and emotionally resonant narratives.

But beware of the seduction of vanity metrics. Impressions, likes, and page views might inflate your ego but look beyond them. Dive into the metrics that translate into business goals—qualified leads, customer acquisition costs, lifetime value—all these tell the story of whether your persuasive tactics are truly hitting home.

Attribution modeling in analytics goes a notch higher, it's the art of pinpointing which touchpoint sways the user toward conversion. It's the strategy that credits the right assist before a goal. Understanding this allows you to allocate resources more effectively, polishing the specific stages of your strategy until they gleam with persuasion.

In summary, analytics serve not just as a mirror reflecting the present but as a crystal ball hinting at future trends. They help predict what topics might resonate and what communication techniques could have a higher persuasion quotient, preparing your arsenal for the next battle even before the current one is won.

Ending this section, it's crucial to understand that the numbers alone aren't the magic wand. It's the interpretation—understanding which levers to pull and which buttons to push—that brings the true magic of persuasion to life. Like a maestro conducting an orchestra, you have to know when to unleash the violins of visual content or the trumpets of compelling copy, all in perfect harmony with the rhythm of your analytics.

Adopting a meticulous, informed approach to analytics empowers digital marketers not just to reach their audiences but to resonate with them. It's this resonance that turns the gears of persuasion, leading to a symphony of marketing success that echoes long after the campaign has ended.

A/B Testing: The Scientific Approach to Persuasion

In the data-driven landscape of digital marketing, the ability to convince and convert rests heavily on understanding what truly resonates with your audience. Enter A/B testing, a methodical approach that can elevate your persuasion strategy from an art to a science. A/B testing, also known as split testing, is the process of comparing two versions of a webpage, email, or other marketing assets to determine which one performs better in terms of your defined conversion goals.

As a master marketer navigating the complexities of the digital domain, you know that gut feeling alone won't suffice. A/B testing provides empirical evidence on what elements of your digital marketing efforts are effective and what needs tweaking. By systematically exposing your audience to variant A or B, you gather data that can't be disputed, and that's the essence of a compelling digital persuasion strategy. After all, what's more persuasive than results that are backed by hard data?

When you set up your A/B test, consider each element that could influence the outcome. This could range from the wording of a call-to-action (CTA) button to the color scheme of a landing page, the image used in an advertisement to the subject line of an email campaign. For A/B testing to effectively guide your persuasion tactics, it's crucial to change only one variable at a time. This way, you can pinpoint exactly which change made the difference in consumer behavior.

A successful A/B test starts with a hypothesis. What do you believe will better persuade your customers: Version A or Version B? You hypothesize, execute, analyze, and then iterate. It's a loop that leads to deeper insights and more nuanced understanding of your audience's preferences and behaviors. Your hypothesis must be clear and based on insights gleaned from previous user data, surveys, or industry trends.

But don't let the simplicity of the concept fool you; nuances in the test design can substantially affect your results. For instance, you'll want to ensure that your audience segments are randomized to avoid selection bias, and that you have a sufficient sample size to reach statistical significance. This ensures the changes you see are due to your tested elements, not random chance.

Once your A/B test is live, practice patience. Running your test for an adequate duration ensures you're capturing enough data to make a reliable decision. This also accounts for any anomalies in user behavior, such as seasonal fluctuations, or unusual traffic spikes due to external factors.

As responses to your A/B test roll in, you'll need to delve into the analytics. But it's not just about the conversion rates. Look at other metrics such as time on page, bounce rate, or click-through rates. Sometimes, the secondary metrics provide invaluable insights that help you understand why one version outperforms the other.

Let's say your A/B test results are in, and you have a winner. What next? Implement the winning element, but don't just stop there; it's time to test again. Digital marketing and user preferences evolve swiftly, and what works today might not work tomorrow. Continuous testing keeps your strategies fresh and relevant.

Remember that even a small percentage increase in conversions can have a significant impact on revenue. This is why A/B testing is considered a cornerstone of optimization for digital marketers. If you're not testing, you're not maximizing your potential to persuade and profit in the digital market space.

Transparency and understanding your audience's reaction to different versions foster trust and credibility. Users appreciate when their feedback is visibly implemented, enhancing their connection to your brand. A company that evolves based on user input is seen as caring and responsive, which is persuasive in itself.

A/B testing transcends simple choice-driven tactics; it becomes a narrative of its own. The data tells a story of what your audience wants and how they want it. Armed with this knowledge, your content, emails, and campaigns become tailored masterpieces that speak directly to your customers' preferences, culminating in higher engagement and conversion rates.

So, think of A/B testing as your digital compass, guiding your marketing efforts towards more compelling and user-focused innovations. By scrutinizing the results of your tests and adapting accordingly, you keep the pulse on the evolving heartbeat of the market. As a result, you develop a marketing strategy that not only persuades but is also perpetually self-improving.

Conclusively, A/B testing isn't just a one-and-done action. It's an ongoing commitment to understanding and shaping the customer experience. It's about making informed decisions that carry substantial weight in guiding your brand towards greater heights of digital persuasion and ultimate market success.

With A/B testing, you're not playing a guessing game; you're harnessing the power of scientific methodology to drive your digital marketing efforts. The results you glean lead to sharper, more effective persuasion techniques that align closely with your audience's needs and preferences. And when you speak directly to what your customers want, using data as your language, you don't just communicate; you connect, convince, and convert with unmatched precision.

Personalization: The Ultimate Persuasion Tool

As we delve deeper into the realm of data-driven persuasion, let's focus on personalization, a cornerstone of modern digital marketing. Personalization is the fine art of tailoring content and experiences to individual users, effectively amplifying the influence of your digital campaigns.

Picture a world where every interaction between your brand and a customer feels like it's custom-crafted. That's the power of personalization: it's like an unseen digital concierge, delivering exactly what your customer wants, possibly even before they realize it themselves.

So, how does one harness this power? It starts with data – the more detailed, the better. Collecting user data such as browsing patterns, purchase history, and engagement levels allows you to understand your customer's preferences and behavior on a granular level.

By leveraging this data through sophisticated algorithms and marketing platforms, you can create individualized user experiences. Let's not forget the importance of maintaining customer trust and privacy while gathering and utilizing data; it's a delicate balance that requires transparency and ethical practices.

Once you have a wealth of data at your fingertips, segmentation takes the stage. It involves dividing your audience into sub-groups based on shared characteristics. This way, you can craft messages that resonate deeply with each group, significantly boosting the relevance and effectiveness of your communication.

Dynamic content is your next instrument in the personalization symphony. It adapts in real time to each user's interactions. Imagine a returning visitor to your site greeted by a banner displaying products related to their previous searches - that's dynamic content in action.

Personalized email marketing campaigns are a testament to the potency of tailored content. Emails using a recipient's name, referencing previous purchases, or suggesting products based on browsing history, consistently perform better in open rates, click-through rates, and sales conversion.

Recommendation engines exemplify personalization by suggesting products or content similar to what the user has already shown interest in. This strategy, popularized by companies like Amazon and Netflix, has proven to skyrocket user engagement and amplify sales.

Let's not overlook the power of personalized storytelling. Create narratives in which your customers see themselves. Use data to speak to their experiences, challenges, and dreams, making your brand's story their story. This establishes an indelible emotional connection that can fortify loyalty and advocacy.

With personalization, timing is everything. The ability to reach customers with the right message at the right time through trigger-based marketing can make the difference between closing a sale and being overlooked. Behavioral triggers such as abandoned carts or visiting a pricing page can be invitations to send personalized, timely messages.

But personalization isn't just about sales. It's about building a lasting relationship. By personalizing customer service interactions and providing tailored support, you can turn customer satisfaction into one of your strongest marketing assets.

Privacy concerns can be a stumbling block. Always prioritize permission-based data collection and comply with regulations such as the General Data Protection Regulation (GDPR). When customers trust you with their data, they expect nothing less than responsible handling. Violating this trust can ruin relationships and tarnish your brand's reputation.

To measure the effectiveness of your personalization efforts, always track your key performance indicators (KPIs) and adjust your strategies based on these analytics. Look out for increases in engagement, conversion rates, customer lifetime value, and retention rates as indicators of personalization success.

Moving forward, it's vital to keep your ear to the ground with the latest in machine learning and artificial intelligence. These technologies are set to advance personalization to staggering new heights, offering unparalleled insights and automation opportunities that we've only just begun to explore.

In conclusion, personalization is not just a tool—it's the ultimate persuasion tool. When done right, it elevates your brand from the noise of the digital landscape and speaks directly to the heart of your audience. Make no mistake, the future of digital marketing is personal, and those who master the art of personalization will lead the charge.

Chapter 8:
The Rise of AI in Digital Marketing

A s we pivot from the empirical approaches of data-driven persuasion explored in the previous chapter, the rising tide of progress ushers us into a new era: the formidable ascent of AI in digital marketing. AI has transcended beyond the realm of sci-fi into a reality of algorithms that can now tailor customer experiences with uncanny finesse and predictive prowess. Within this transformative landscape, the art of persuasion becomes augmented by machine learning models that dissect vast troves of data to unearth individual preferences, serving up content and interactions that resonate on a personal level. With AI, marketers are no longer casting wide nets, but threading needles with precision—anticipating needs, optimizing touchpoints, and engaging audiences with a newfound dynamism that propels conversions. The savviest of professionals recognize AI as not just a tool, but a collaborator in crafting narratives that entice and retain, forging ahead in an ever-evolving digital bazaar where the only constant is innovation.

AI-Powered Content Creation: Next-Level Personalization

The advent of artificial intelligence has marked the beginning of a transformative era in digital marketing. Its integration into content creation offers an unparalleled potential for personalization that breathes new life into the dynamic between brands and their audiences. In this chapter, we delve into the fascinating possibilities that AI-fueled content strategies present to businesses who are eager to stay at the forefront of digital engagement.

Imagine crafting content that resonates with each individual on a deeply personal level, scaling these individualized experiences without sacrificing the quality or the essence of the brand's voice. This is not merely a futuristic dream—it's the current landscape for marketers who harness the power of AI in their content creation.

AI-driven content tools are not just about automation; they're about understanding and anticipating the needs and interests of your audience. With advanced algorithms, AI can sift through vast amounts of data to pinpoint patterns and preferences, allowing you to cater content directly to the user's journey—turning every touchpoint into an opportunity to captivate and persuade.

Personalization goes beyond using a customer's name. It's about creating a content experience that feels specifically designed for the user, from the topics discussed to the timing of the delivery. AI can analyze past behavior to predict future interests, generating content that users didn't even realize they were seeking but find irresistibly relevant.

This technology enables the dynamic customization of content. Whether it's an email, a landing page, or a social media post, AI can tweak the message to best suit the user who is engaging with it. The potential for A/B testing is exponentially increased, allowing marketers to quickly learn what works on a micro-scale and adjust in real-time for maximum persuasion and impact.

Targeted content also supports the critical principle of scarcity. AI's predictive capabilities can pinpoint the optimum moments to present limited-offer promotions to those most likely to perceive their value, drastically improving conversion rates.

Coupled with the six principles of influence outlined earlier in the book, AI can amplify the effect of tactics like reciprocity and authority. For instance, AI can generate informative blog posts tailored to answer specific questions for different user segments, thereby not only providing value upfront but also cementing the brand's position as an authority within its niche.

Consistency in brand messaging is another aspect drastically improved by AI. Imagine a world where your brand voice is unfailingly coherent, yet each message is uniquely fine-tuned for the person reading it. Such seamless integration of consistency and personalization was once a digital marketer's pipe dream, but with AI, it's becoming daily practice.

We must consider the role that AI content creation plays in understanding the social proof principle. By analyzing social data, AI can highlight trending topics, common questions, and the prevailing sentiment around a brand, enabling the creation of content that engages at the precise intersection of social conversation and brand relevance.

Throughout this exploration into AI-driven personalization, it's crucial to maintain an element of human touch. Knowing how to blend the efficiency and intelligence of AI with the creativity and empathy of human experience is the key balance that marketers must strive for. While AI can provide the tools for personalization, it still requires the marketer's strategic vision to guide it.

As we integrate AI into content creation workflows, we mustn't lose sight of the story we are telling. Yes, AI can craft a perfectly optimized headline or suggest the next viral topic, but it is the marketer's duty to ensure that the narrative remains authentic, engaging, and true to the brand ethos.

AI-powered content creation is reshaping the digital landscape, making next-level personalization not just a possibility but an expectation among consumers. It's an exciting journey that empowers marketers to create more meaningful and impactful engagements with their audience, forging stronger connections and driving brand loyalty.

By unlocking the full potential of AI-powered content, marketers open the door to a world where each click and interaction gets transformed into a deeply personal brand experience. It's an opportunity to not just be a part of the customer's world but to integrate into it seamlessly, paving the way for the future of digital persuasion.

Sailing this new digital sea requires a deft hand and an understanding of how these tools can be used ethically and effectively. As AI continues to evolve, it's vital for marketers to stay informed, adaptive, and always mindful of the power they wield. It's not an overstatement to say that AI-powered content creation has become an indispensable component of a strong digital marketing strategy.

The innovative use of AI in content creation is both a challenge and an opportunity for digital marketers. As we move forward, embracing these technologies will not just be beneficial—it will be essential for creating compelling, persuasive content that stands out in an ever-crowded digital marketplace. In the next sections, we'll explore further how AI facilitates conversational marketing through chatbots and how predictive analytics can take anticipation of audience needs to an entirely new level.

Chatbots and Conversational Marketing

In the profound transition that digitization has heralded for marketing, one development stands to reshape the landscape further: AI-powered chatbots and conversational marketing. Embracing the vanguard of customer interaction, this technology hands marketers the ability to engage in personal conversations with thousands of customers simultaneously, providing instant support and forging stronger customer relationships.

Chatbots are redefining customer service as we know it, operating on the front lines to answer queries, gather data, and guide users through the sales funnel. They merge the potent principles of convenience with personalized interaction, creating a seamless bridge between customers and the services they seek. This harmonious blend of immediate utility with a human-like touch equips marketers with an invaluable tool to captivate customers' interest.

As they stand today, these AI-driven assistants aren't just scripts that regurgitate pre-defined answers. Instead, they learn from each interaction to better understand and respond to the subtleties of human language. This evolution allows them to approach the nuance of human converse increasingly close, making each interaction feel less mechanical and more empathetic.

These AI conversationalists are available around the clock, providing customers with uninterrupted service—a luxury that human personnel can seldom afford. This ensures that when a potential customer is browsing your site at an odd hour, they're still receiving immediate attention, fostering a sense of being valued and heard.

Marketers are well aware that time is of the essence in the digital world. The fast response time of chatbots means that customer queries aren't just answered: they're answered promptly, which reduces bounce rates and increases the likelihood of conversion. In a digital era that highly values speed, chatbots ensure your brand keeps pace with the rapidity of customer expectations.

However, it's not solely about answering questions. Chatbots excel in engaging users by using persuasive language tailored to the user's input and previous behavior. They indeed act as a persuasive force, ushering users gently towards the yawn of the conversion funnel with interactions that feel remarkably human.

Utilizing chatbots for conversational marketing effortlessly taps into multiple principles of influence simultaneously. For example, chatbot interactions personalized to each user can create a sense of reciprocity: the user feels the brand has invested time and effort into assisting them, compelling them to reciprocate by considering the brand's products or services.

Moreover, AI development has enabled chatbots to manage more sophisticated tasks, such as resolving complex customer service issues or guiding a customer through a personalized shopping experience. Such advancements deepen the customer-brand relationship, reinforcing the commitment and consistency in brand messaging.

Remarkably, chatbots don't operate in isolation. They can be seamlessly integrated into social media platforms, projecting your influence through the channels where your customers spend the majority of their digital time. Instant Messaging apps, social media platforms, and even your website can house these chatbots to engage and persuade potential customers.

One can't overlook the benefit of data collection and analytics that chatbots offer. With each conversation, they aggregate valuable customer insights—preferences, behaviors, and feedback—which can be used to refine marketing strategies. This data allows for a more personalized experience for the user and more targeted and persuasive marketing efforts.

The integration of chatbots into a larger digital strategy shouldn't be seen merely as an addition but as a transformation. They redefine the sales and service environment with conversational marketing being the focus—making engagements with users more dynamic, insightful, and resulting in a smoothened path to purchase.

Deploying chatbots is also a nod towards future-proofing your digital marketing strategy. As AI technology evolves, so too will the capabilities and sophistication of conversational agents. Early adoption paves the way for businesses to stay ahead of the curve, capitalizing on technological advancements as they roll out.

In embracing chatbots, businesses and marketers launch into the world of conversational marketing—a space where connections are forged stronger and conversion pathways are etched clearer. It's an arena where persuasive communication can be scaled, where every customer can feel like they're in a one-on-one conversation with your brand, even when they're one of thousands.

Finally, it's vital to instill in these digital interlocutors a voice that aligns seamlessly with your brand's messaging and values. Developing a chatbot with a personality and responses that echo your company's tone and ethos ensures a consistent and authentic experience for users, further solidifying their image of your business as one that understands and cares about their needs.

Conversational marketing, particularly through chatbots, is a powerful amplifier of your brand's voice and a persuasive tool that bridges gaps between technology and sincere human interaction. It is an investment into building lasting relationships, converting curious visitors into loyal customers, and ensuring that the complexities of human conversation are not lost in the digital marketing conquest.

Predictive Analytics: Anticipating Your Audience's Needs

In an age where digital space is saturated with content, standing out requires not only creativity but also a strategic understanding of your audience's needs. This is where predictive analytics enters the scene, offering digital marketers a futurist's lens to anticipate demands, preferences, and behaviors. The marriage of artificial intelligence and marketing data has birthed a powerhouse capable of not just reacting to trends but foreseeing them. And for you—an innovator, a strategist, a marketer—this marks the beginning of a new chapter in digital persuasion.

Predictive analytics does not rest solely on one's intuition but on a blend of data-driven insights and anticipatory modeling that reveals what the audience might crave next. We are now witness to marketing's clairvoyance, where AI algorithms process historical data, consumer interactions, and buying habits to forecast future outcomes. These predictive models become the compass guiding campaigns, tailoring messages that resonate with audiences before they even articulate their desires.

By harnessing the power of predictive analytics, you can map out a customer's journey with greater precision. Each step a user takes—be it a click, a download, or a purchase—feeds into an evolving database. The AI, ever-learning, tweaks its predictions, refining the path to conversion with each interaction. It's not about casting a wide net but about stitching a tailored suit—one that fits the market's shifting contours snugly.

The use of predictive analytics is multifold. It sharpens targeting, enhances content relevance, and optimizes resource allocation. Picture your email marketing campaigns becoming more nuanced, sending out messages aligned not just with where your audience has been, but where they're most likely heading. By forecasting which topics will garner interest, you can prime your calendar with discussions, content, and offers that meet your audience at the crossroads of curiosity and necessity.

To effectively deploy predictive analytics, one must first delve into the wealth of existing customer data—mining insights from past interactions and behaviors. This initial step is critical, as it sets the groundwork upon which predictive models are built. Remember, the foundation for predicting the future lies in understanding the past. The richer the historical data, the clearer the future becomes.

Data segmentation plays an essential role in this predictive journey. By categorizing your audience into distinct groups based on demographics, psychographics, and buying patterns, AI can furnish each segment with the most enticing messages and offers. These are not generic broadcasts but targeted transmissions designed to engage and persuade at an individual level.

In the realm of content creation, AI-driven predictive analytics empowers you to deliver customized experiences. Whether it's a blog post, social media update, or product recommendation, the content that gleams with prescient knowledge can captivate and convert with remarkable effectiveness. This kind of personalization is not a frivolous embellishment but a strategic imperative in a market where the average consumer's attention is a prize fought over by countless contenders.

Moreover, predictive analytics elevates the efficiency of A/B testing, transforming it from a tool that confirms hunches to one that generates proactive insights. Imagine being able to test future scenarios based on predictions and adjust your marketing efforts before fully rolling them out. It's an iterative process of hypothesize, test, and refine that propels campaigns forward with the momentum of certainty.

Consider also the role of AI in managing and adjusting campaigns in real-time. Predictive models rapidly process incoming data, allowing marketing efforts to be agile—shifting gears and adapting creatives in response to unfolding trends. It's the closest thing to having a crystal ball, and in this high-speed digital marketplace, it's akin to having superpowers.

But predictive analytics is not a silver bullet. It requires discernment and a thoughtful approach. The data may point you in a direction, but as a skilled marketer, you need to navigate with an understanding of your brand's voice and ethical standards. Predictions should be balanced with intuition and human creativity, ensuring that while data may inform your decision, it doesn't override the authenticity of your brand's message.

Furthermore, approaching predictive analytics necessitates a partnership between marketers and data scientists. The collaboration is paramount to not only interpret the data but also to craft stories from the numbers that reflect the 'human' in the digital experience. It's a dance between logic and emotion, between algorithm and narrative.

Anticipating your audience's needs also means staying ahead of technological advancements. Staying informed about the latest tools and methodologies in predictive analytics will ensure that your strategies remain cutting-edge and effective. Lifelong learning is not an option in this field; it's a requirement.

Lastly, while predictive analytics offers a gateway to the audience's future needs, it's also essential to maintain an ongoing conversation with them. Engage with your community, seek feedback, and listen to the voices that interact with your brand. These real-world inputs validate and augment the predictions, ensuring that your strategy maintains its relevance and resonance.

As you journey through the evolving landscape of digital marketing, armed with the prowess of predictive analytics, let your vision be clear. You're not just chasing the present but sculpting the future. Each campaign you launch, powered by the foresight of AI, is an opportunity to demonstrate your brand's empathy, agility, and innovation. So channel the insights at your disposal to speak directly to the hearts and minds of your audience, and watch as predictive analytics transforms uncertainty into unprecedented growth and connection.

Chapter 9:
Influencer Marketing and Collaborations

Venturing deeper into the realm of digital connections, Chapter 9 illuminates the powerful strategy of Influencer Marketing and Collaborations. Imagine leveraging the charismatic pull of influential figures to sway public opinion and elevate your brand's visibility. This approach isn't just about choosing a figure with a colossal following; it's about pinpointing personalities whose values align seamlessly with your brand, creating a mutual boost in credibility and reach. As your journey into influencer marketing unfolds, you'll grasp the intricacies of identifying influencers who resonate with your audience, mapping out campaigns that capitalize on shared goals, and engage in collaborative storytelling that feels authentic and transparent. The bond you craft with these influencers becomes the bridge to a wider audience, an audience that's predisposed to trust their endorsement. In the fusion of two marketing forces, there's a synergy that could catapult your brand to new heights—provided that you maintain a clear ethical compass, ensuring that every influencer partnership nurtures trust and delivers genuine value. By mastering the art of influencer collaborations, you position your brand at the forefront of a networked world, where authority is voiced through the dynamic interplay of shared influence and collective ambition.

Identifying and Partnering with Key Influencers

In the fluid realm of influencer marketing, navigating the waters to find and partner with key influencers is akin to discovering an uncharted territory that promises immense opportunities. It's an intricate dance of identifying voices that resonate authentically with your brand and cultivating relationships that lead to successful collaborations. This endeavor requires a precise mix of research, strategy, and interpersonal skills to capture the collective imagination of your audience.

Initially, the pursuit to find the right influencer begins with a crystal-clear understanding of your brand's core identity and the audience segments you intend to reach. Picture your ideal influencer as a mirror reflection of your brand's values, aesthetic, and ethos. In this light, influencers aren't just endorsers—they become the human touchpoint between your brand and your audience, engaging them in a narrative that feels both genuine and compelling.

Embarking on this quest mandates that you leverage the power of social listening. Dive into the digital depths of conversations, trends, hashtags, and communities to scout for influencers who not only speak to your audience but also engage them in ways that stir a brand-aligned dialogue. Tools and platforms specializing in social media analytics can provide invaluable information to map out the influence landscape relevant to your brand.

Differentiation is pivotal. Acknowledge that influencers span a wide spectrum, from the industry-celebrated, with followers in the millions, known as mega-influencers, to the niche micro-influencers who boast higher engagement rates within a tightly-knit community. Deciding on a partnership with either comes down to your campaign objectives, whether it's broad-reaching awareness or deep, targeted engagement.

Once you've zeroed in on potential influencers, it's time to engage in due diligence. A deep dive into the historical content of influencers provides insight into consistency, brand affinity, and the authenticity of their engagements. Scrutinize the landscape for red flags like inflated follower counts or engagement metrics that don't stack up. Remember, the quality of the influencer's engagement often trumps the quantity of their audience.

Engaging in initial conversations with influencers requires tact and respect for their craft. As breeders of content, influencers appreciate creative freedom. Your proposal should intrinsically understand and respect their content style and give them the liberty to express your brand message in a way that maintains their original voice. This collaboration should feel less like an acquisition and more like a partnership.

Constructing compelling pitch ideas is key to capturing the interest of an influencer. Make it transparent why a partnership would benefit both parties. Tailor your pitch to highlight shared values and potential growth opportunities while demonstrating knowledge of the influencer's work. Remember, influencers are often pitched multiple times a day; distinctiveness will make your proposition stand out.

Having identified the right match, the art of negotiation begins. Influencers, like any other professionals, seek fair compensation for their work. Discussions about money can be delicate, so approach these with clarity and professionalism. Consider not only direct financial compensation but also other forms of value exchange, such as exclusive access to products or events, that can sweeten the deal.

Contractual clarity cannot be overstated when cementing influencer partnerships. Contracts should outline expectations, deliverables, timelines, rights usage, and any other specifics pertinent to the collaboration. This step safeguards both parties' interests and sets up a clear roadmap for the partnership to flourish without ambiguity.

Once the partnership kicks off, it's essential to maintain open lines of communication. Active engagement and responsiveness serve as the support system for influencers to feel valued and understood. This ensures they are equipped to represent your brand in the best light and can adapt to any evolving campaign needs or audience responses.

Measuring the impact of influencer partnerships isn't just a post-campaign activity. Establish benchmarks and KPIs early on—be it reach, engagement, conversions, or brand sentiment—that align with your marketing objectives. Regularly analyze campaign data to understand performance and leverage these insights for ongoing optimization.

The dynamic nature of influencer collaborations demands flexibility. Be prepared to iterate based on real-time learnings, and allow influencers to be co-creators in adapting the campaign. Sometimes the most valuable insights come from the influencers' firsthand experience with their audience, which can guide your brand towards more impactful strategies.

One must not forget the importance of nurturing long-term relationships with influencers. Beyond individual campaigns, there's immense value in building a network of influencers who become brand advocates. These enduring partnerships can create a bedrock of trust and reliance, paving the way for future collaborations and deeper audience penetration.

In the pursuit of identifying and partnering with key influencers, approach the process with a blend of analytical rigor and human touch. Each step, from research and outreach to negotiation and execution, is a testament to the power of building bridges between your brand and your audience through the conduit of influential voices. When these partnerships are forged with strategy and sincerity, the resonance is amplified across the digital tapestry, setting the stage for marketing that not only persuades but mesmerizes.

Remember, the right influencer collaboration is not just about who has the loudest voice, but who speaks your brand's language with an authenticity that captivates and converts. This journey, filled with opportunities for growth, learning, and impactful connections, lies at the heart of modern digital marketing, driving forward with a synergy that leaves indelible marks on the digital landscape.

Crafting Campaigns for Co-Marketing Success

Co-marketing is a symphony of strategy and synergy. When businesses collaborate with one another, especially alongside influencers, they can create campaigns that leverage the strengths of each partner to achieve greater marketing success. In the realm of influencer collaborations, co-marketing takes on a whole new dimension. It combines the clout and reach of influencers with the expertise and resources of brands to forge campaigns that resonate deeply with target audiences. But how does one craft such campaigns that not only capture attention but also convert?

The starting point is always a deep understanding of the combined audience. To shape a campaign that truly impacts the marketplace, it's imperative to know who you are speaking to. This involves a granular analysis of both the brand's and the influencer's followers. What common interests do they share? Where does the overlap in their values lie? Identifying these intersections sets the stage for messaging that strikes a chord.

Next, the alignment of goals is crucial. Both parties must share a vision for what the campaign aims to achieve—whether it's raising brand awareness, launching a new product, or driving sales. Clear objectives pave the way for focused strategies that keep both teams on the same page. And when goals align, each partner can contribute in ways that highlight their strengths, leading to more authentic, effective campaigns.

A co-marketing masterpiece is built on the foundation of a compelling story. Here, the art of crafting narratives comes into play. The campaign should weave together the brand ethos with the influencer's personality. It's not just about promoting a product or service; it's about creating a storyline that audiences can connect with on an emotional level. This narrative must be both authentic and engaging, ensuring the storyline resonates with the audience's own experiences and aspirations.

Communication is the lifeblood of any successful collaboration. Throughout the campaign, maintaining open channels for feedback and adaptation is essential. With the digital landscape rapidly evolving, being able to pivot and tweak campaign elements in real-time is a valuable asset. This adaptive approach can make the difference between a campaign that fizzles out and one that flourishes.

When diving into the nuts and bolts, creative brainstorming sessions are where the magic happens. Here, ideas are exchanged, concepts are hatched, and innovative solutions are found. It's important to create a space where creativity is not just welcomed but encouraged—a breeding ground for the unique selling points that will differentiate the campaign in a cluttered market.

Variety in content format is another powerful element in crafting co-marketing campaigns. Combining educational blog posts, emotional storytelling, eye-catching social media content, and impactful videos can cater to different audience preferences, ensuring that the campaign has multiple touchpoints. Diverse content forms not only engage users in different ways but also help in maximizing the exposure across platforms.

Exclusivity thrives in co-marketing campaigns. Offering something unique that can't be found elsewhere—a limited edition product, a special service bundle, or access to exclusive content—creates a sense of privilege among the target audience. This not only drives immediate engagement but also fosters a long-term association with both the influencer and the brand.

Timing is everything. Launching campaigns when they are most likely to be noticed requires strategic planning. This includes understanding social media algorithms, posting schedules, and even coordinating with cultural or seasonal events that complement the campaign's theme. A well-timed campaign maximizes reach and captivates attention when audiences are most receptive.

Metrics and KPIs lend a factual edge to the creative process. By setting measurable targets, both the influencer and the brand can track progress and measure the impact of their efforts. What's more, analyzing these metrics will provide valuable insights for optimizing the campaign's performance and informing future collaborations.

To amplify the campaign's reach, sponsored content and paid advertising can be employed tactically. While organic reach is important, supplementing it with paid efforts can expand the visibility of the campaign significantly. Strategic ad placements and promotions guided by data-driven decisions can ensure that the campaign gets in front of the right eyes.

No campaign should end abruptly. Sustained engagement post-campaign is necessary to solidify the connection made with the audience. This could mean continued interaction through comments, follow-up content, or even aftersales support. It shows the audience that the partnership between the brand and the influencer wasn't a one-off event but a genuine and lasting relationship.

Legal compliance and ethical considerations must be part of the early planning stages. This includes transparent disclosure of the partnership, respecting copyright laws, and ensuring that all promotional messaging is truthful. Trust is at the cornerstone of any partnership, and adherence to these guidelines is critical in maintaining credibility with the audience.

Innovation in co-marketing campaigns helps redefine what collaboration means. Experimenting with new platforms, technologies, and communication techniques keeps campaigns fresh and engaging. The digital landscape is dynamic, and staying ahead of the curve with innovative approaches can make a campaign stand out.

The importance of a solid follow-through strategy cannot be overstated. Capturing leads, nurturing them through the sales funnel, and eventually converting them requires consistent effort. The campaign might be the hook, but the follow-through will reel in the catch. This means extensive planning from the very first contact point all the way to the final conversion.

Last but not least, evaluation is key to future success. After each campaign, take a step back and analyze the outcomes. What worked well? What didn't? What could be improved? Every campaign is a learning opportunity—one that provides precious insights that can shape the success of subsequent campaigns. By learning from each experience, brands and influencers can refine their strategies, sharpen their messaging, and forge an ever-stronger bond with their audience.

Co-marketing success relies on a delicate balance of partnership, strategy, and execution. By crafting campaigns that embody this triad, brands and influencers can harness the full power of collaboration. It's through insightful planning, cohesive storytelling, and relentless innovation that the most memorable and effective co-marketing campaigns are born.

The Ethics of Influence: Transparency and Authenticity

In the fast-evolving realm of digital marketing, one of the robust veins that pumps vitality into a brand's image is influencer marketing. It's not just about capitalizing on an influencer's audience but about crafting a relationship based on transparency and authenticity.

At the heart of any successful influencer collaboration lies a mutual understanding of ethical practice. Transparency isn't merely a buzzword to toss around when convenient. It's an uncompromising cornerstone of trust between brands, influencers, and their audiences. When an influencer genuinely believes in a product or service, their endorsements are authentic, providing tangible value to their followers.

Golden threads of authenticity should be woven throughout any narrative your brand shares. When influencers mirror these sentiments, their audience receives the message as credible and trustworthy. Authenticity spurs a powerful emotional connection, urging followers to consider, engage with, and ultimately trust your brand.

As you embark on influencer campaigns, steer clear of murky waters where undisclosed partnerships and disingenuous recommendations lurk. Federal Trade Commission (FTC) guidelines necessitate the clear and conspicuous disclosure of partnerships. Non-compliance can not only tarnish a brand's image but also result in hefty penalties.

For digital marketers, fostering clear disclosure habits within influencer relations is vital. Audiences should never be left guessing if a recommendation is born out of genuine appreciation or a paid partnership. Inform your influencers about the importance of #ad or #sponsored tags and ensure they understand the implications of non-disclosure.

Another key component of ethical influencer marketing is alignment—ensuring that the influencer's values and audience match those of your brand. This symphony of values resonates with consumers, yielding a more engaging and effective campaign. Forced partnerships can appear disingenuous, pushing consumers towards skepticism instead of loyalty.

While building partnerships, remember that influencers are much more than just marketing channels. They are brand ambassadors and should be empowered to share their true experiences. Scripted messages are instantly recognizable and can detract from the perceived authenticity of the partnership.

Despite the temptation to control every aspect of the communication, brands should find comfort in organic, unscripted content that influencers share, provided it aligns with the overall messaging and objectives. This space for creativity and individual interpretation feeds into the influencer's personal brand, enhancing the receptivity of the campaign.

Quality trumps quantity. A smaller but more engaged and dedicated following can often provide more value than a vast but disengaged audience. Micro-influencers, for example, tend to have higher engagement rates and their endorsements typically come across as more authentic due to the close-knit nature of their communities.

Always vet potential influencer partners through a lens of integrity. Investigate past partnerships, the consistency of their content, and how they interact with their audience. This diligence ensures that the influencer you partner with can genuinely advocate for your brand, ultimately reinforcing trust.

It's imperative to bear in mind the lifespan of digital content. Transparency and authenticity don't expire once the campaign ends. Enduring respect and admiration from consumers stem from consistent, ethical marketing practices. Regular evaluations and refreshers on ethical standards for both your brand and your collaborators can maintain this adherence.

By embracing ethical practices in influencer collaborations, you not only protect your brand's reputation but also contribute to a more trustworthy digital marketing ecosystem. Your audience grows to expect transparency as a given and begins to value authenticity in every part of their online experience. In turn, they become loyal champions of your brand, spreading the word far and wide with genuine enthusiasm.

Let us challenge the narrative that influencer marketing lacks depth and substance. Influencer partnerships can, and should, be rich in meaning and purpose, punctuated by the pillars of transparency and authenticity. This strategy not only honors the intelligence and discernment of the modern consumer but sets a standard for ethical digital persuasion.

Remember, your audience is sophisticated and perceptive. They can sense the difference between tactful influence and deceptive manipulation. By upholding the highest standards of ethical conduct in all your influencer marketing endeavors, you earn the respect and trust that are essential to long-term success in the ever-changing landscape of the digital world.

Chapter 10:
Engagement and Community Building

In the dynamic world of digital marketing, the art of engagement and the craft of community building are the twin pillars that transform passive onlookers into active participants and brand advocates. As we delve into the rich tapestry of interactive content, we unlock the potential of each click, like, and share to forge deeper connections with our audience. Envision hosting webinars and live sessions that aren't just broadcasts but communal experiences, where every question asked is an opportunity to add a personal touch, and every answer given strengthens the bond of community. The journey of building a brand community is much like tending to a vibrant garden; it requires patience, nurturing, and an understanding of the ecosystem to bloom fully. As we cultivate this digital landscape, each member becomes a seed of possibility, ready to grow into a loyal customer or an influential brand ambassador. In this chapter, we will guide you through the intricacies of fostering meaningful interactions and constructing a community that resonates with the heart of your brand, turning engagement into a powerful catalyst for growth.

Interactive Content: Engaging Your Audience

Stepping into the realm of digital marketing means accepting the challenge of how to continuously engage your audience. Building connections in the digital space is about starting conversations, sparking curiosity, and maintaining a dynamic presence that thrives on user interaction. Today, we're exploring the compelling world of interactive content and its pivotal role in hooking your audience's attention.

Interactive content isn't just a fleeting trend; it's becoming a cornerstone of user engagement. No longer can digital marketers rely solely on static posts or generic updates. The bar has been raised, and the expectation is for content that prompts action—content that makes your audience sit up, take notice, and participate.

Let's dissect the myriad forms that interactive content can take. From quizzes and polls to interactive infographics, these are more than just tools—they're experiences. A well-crafted quiz can lead a user down a path of personalized discovery, subtly aligning them with your brand's solutions. Polls, on the other hand, are not mere indicators of public opinion; they are powerful conversation starters and data mines, gathered in real-time for your strategic analysis.

Think about the potential of immersive experiences like augmented and virtual reality. They may sound like futuristic concepts, but they're here, and they're reshaping how brands and consumers connect. Imagine inviting someone to virtually try out your product from the comfort of their home or providing an augmented reality tour of your facility. Such experiences don't just tell; they show, and in doing so, they forge deeper emotional connections with the users.

Then there are interactive videos, a leap beyond passive viewing, where users dictate the narrative through their choices. Shoppable videos have even entered the fray, allowing viewers to make purchases directly from the multimedia content they are watching. This seamless integration of storytelling and commerce is redefining the very concept of engaging content.

For the digital marketer, creating this interactive content isn't simply about piquing interest; it's also about gathering the valuable data that these engagements provide. Every click, choice, and interaction is a goldmine of insights into your audience's preferences, behaviors, and desires. Leveraging this data means crafting content that's increasingly tailored and targeted, revving up the persuasive power of your digital strategy.

Now, what makes interactive content truly impactful? Personalization. It transforms the generic to the specific, whispering directly to the user's individual needs and aspirations. Personalized recommendations, for instance, not only save the user time but also demonstrate an understanding of their unique challenges and how your brand can provide the solution.

Don't miss out on the opportunity to integrate interactive elements into your email campaigns. By inviting recipients to engage within the email itself, you reduce barriers to participation. Picture an interactive newsletter where readers can rate articles or a product email where they can customize their order without leaving their inbox—the possibilities are as innovative as they are effective.

Gamification is another dimension of interactive content that can't be overlooked. It adds a layer of motivation and competition, whether through collecting points, unlocking achievements, or climbing leaderboards. Users aren't just casual observers; they become active participants eagerly returning for more.

To ensure your interactive content hits the mark, you must keep user experience at the forefront. Content that is clunky or overly complex will deter rather than engage. Every interactive element must be effortless to navigate, intuitive in design, and accessible across devices and platforms.

However, engagement doesn't end when the user finishes the interaction. The follow-up is equally vital. Whether it's a thank-you message, a summary of insights gleaned from their responses, or suggestions for further exploration, closing the interaction loop ensures that users feel valued and seen.

Moreover, interactive content can become a breeding ground for community discussion. Results of quizzes can be shared, poll results can be debated, and unique experiences can be recounted amongst peers on social media and forums. Each interaction sparks a potential conversation about your brand and its offerings.

But with all these tools at your fingertips, remember that moderation is key. Not every piece of content needs to be interactive. Aim for a balance in your content strategy. Diverse content types ensure that your audience never tires of one particular form. It keeps them guessing, intrigued, and eager for what's next from your brand.

Finally, revisiting and refining your approach to interactive content is essential. As with all digital marketing strategies, what works today may not work tomorrow. Keep a keen eye on metrics, be ready to pivot, and always, always prioritize delivering value to the user. Excellence in interactive content isn't just about flashy technology— it's about meaningful engagement that nurtures lasting relationships with your audience.

In wrapping up this exploration of interactive content, it's clear that the heart of engagement lies in creating memorable, meaningful interactions. As we venture further into the digital age, the power to captivate and connect with our audience through interactive content will continue to shape the landscape of digital marketing. Harness this potential, and you're well on your way to fostering a space where your brand and your community can thrive together.

Hosting Webinars and Live Sessions

In the pursuit of deepening engagement and fortifying community bonds, hosting webinars and live sessions stand out as critical tools for the savvy digital marketer. These platforms offer an unparalleled opportunity to interact directly with your audience, providing a space where participants can feel seen, heard, and valued. The immediacy of live interaction facilitates a stronger connection between you and your community, amplifying the reach and resonance of your message.

To begin, understand that webinars are more than just presentations; they are interactive experiences. The first step is to select a topic that not only sparks interest but also provides unmistakable value to your audience. Consider addressing prevalent challenges or hot topics within your industry, as doing so will naturally attract a crowd eager for insights and solutions. Moreover, it highlights your brand's commitment to contributing value, thereby leveraging the principle of reciprocity in your digital content.

When planning your webinar, make its structure flexible enough to include a Q&A segment. This segment is the cornerstone of community engagement during the live session. It opens up a dialogue and allows participants to have their specific questions addressed, fostering a sense of individual attention that can form the bedrock of loyalty to your brand.

Promotion is the key. Utilize every digital channel at your disposal to announce your live sessions. Email invitations, social media posts, and even countdowns can build anticipation. Highlighting the exclusive nature of the content you'll be sharing taps into the scarcity principle, making it an irresistible event for your target audience.

The technical aspect of hosting a webinar should not be overlooked. Ensure you have reliable software that supports seamless presentation delivery, audience participation features, and recording capabilities. A clean, high-quality stream with minimal technical hitches speaks volumes about your brand's professionalism and competence.

Engagement doesn't stop with the live session. Recorded webinars can extend the life of your content, serve as a resource for those who missed the live event, and attract new viewers. This is where the commitment and consistency principle helps your brand messaging; offering a consistent schedule or archive of webinars makes your brand a reliable source of information.

Personalization can significantly boost the impact of your webinars. Addressing attendees by name, if possible, or segmenting your audience to tailor the session more closely to their interests, can heighten their sense of connection to your brand. Remind yourself that live sessions are not just about disseminating information; they're about creating a shared experience.

Interactive elements such as polls, surveys, and interactive Q&A sessions enliven your webinar and provide valuable feedback. These tools are also an excellent way to collect data about your audience's preferences and pain points, which can inform future marketing strategies or content creation.

The storytelling technique is a potent tool during webinars. Weave in narratives that resonate with your audience's aspirations and challenges. A story that illustrates your message or showcases a customer's journey can punctuate the factual content with emotion, rendering it more memorable and persuasive.

Don't neglect the power of follow-up. After your live session, reach out to the participants with a thank you message, a survey for feedback, or an exclusive offer. This post-webinar engagement can cement the relationship between your brand and your audience, and encourage future interactions.

Hosting webinars and live sessions also provides an opportunity to demonstrate authority in your domain. Your audience is looking not just for information but for expertise and trusted advice. Use this platform to showcase your knowledge, experience, and unique perspective on the subject matter.

While the content is primary, the delivery is just as significant. A dynamic and engaging presenter can hold the audience's attention, drive home key messages, and leave a lasting impression. Invest in developing presentation skills, whether that means honing them yourself or bringing in talented speakers who can captivate and educate your audience.

Leveraging the power of social proof during live sessions can also be incredibly effective. Featuring testimonials or case studies during the webinar validates your claims and showcases the success others have had with your brand. It's the digital equivalent of word-of-mouth marketing, wherein real stories instill a sense of trust and reliability in your offering.

Finally, recognize the importance of adaptability. Feedback from your audience and the performance of each session should inform the development of future webinars. Iteration is vital; use what works, discard what doesn't, and always be on the lookout for ways to enhance the value and effectiveness of your live sessions.

In the end, the success of webinars and live sessions in building a community lies in the capacity to engage authentically, consistently, and persuasively with your audience. Each session is an opportunity to reinforce your brand's message, deepen connections, and drive home the value that your brand provides. It's a platform not just for broadcasting your voice but for starting a conversation—one that has the potential to grow into a community of brand advocates and loyal customers.

Building a Brand Community

In the modern tapestry of digital marketing, fostering a robust brand community stands as a beacon of thriving engagement. At its core, a brand community is a specialized, non-geographically bound community, based on a structured set of social relations among admirers of a brand. This gathering of individuals with shared interests and values offers an unparalleled opportunity to cultivate loyalty, create advocates, and generate invaluable human connections. Understanding how to build and nurture this community is pivotal for brands seeking to solidify their presence and influence in today's digital landscape.

To embark on the journey of building a brand community, begin by clearly defining your brand's purpose and values. These are the magnetic forces that will attract like-minded individuals to your orbit. A brand without compelling values or a clear purpose can seldom inspire the formation of a community since there is no shared belief that binds its members together. Explicitly communicate your mission and vision through every digital interaction. Consistency in this message reinforces the community's foundation upon which all engagement rests.

Strengthening the sense of community involves the creation of an exclusive space where your brand enthusiasts can congregate. This could be a forum on your website, a dedicated Facebook group or a hashtag that aggregates content on social media channels. The aim is to provide a platform where conversations can flourish and where members can connect with one another. These spaces should be carefully monitored and guided to foster positive and supportive interactions.

When considering the architecture of your community, prioritize a top-notch user experience. Seamlessly navigable platforms, engaging content, and responsive design ensure that community members enjoy their time within your digital ecosystem. This level of care communicates that you value their participation and fosters a deeper emotional connection with your brand.

Engagement is the currency of community building. It's not enough to simply gather individuals; one should strive to captivate them with compelling content, conversation starters, and opportunities for participation. Encourage user-generated content to shine a spotlight on your community members and make them feel like an integral part of the brand's narrative. Recognizing your members not just as customers but as co-creators and contributors can forge a powerful bond.

Mark the importance of interaction by being an active participant in your own community. Respond to comments, acknowledge feedback, and celebrate community achievements. Such responsiveness signifies that you're not just a brand talking at consumers but talking with them. Being present and available fosters a sense of trust and reliability that is quintessential for community cohesion.

Intensity in your community management efforts can elevate the quality of interactions and the satisfaction of community members. Appointing a dedicated community manager or team ensures that someone is always tending to the pulse of the community, spotting trends, addressing issues, and capitalizing on engagement opportunities.

Leverage events to stir excitement and draw your community closer together. Organize live Q&A sessions, webinars, or online workshops that provide value and encourage real-time interaction. Such events not only serve as knowledge sharing platforms but also as an avenue for members to solidify their loyalty and for you to showcase the human side of your brand.

Rewarding community engagement with recognition programs, exclusive content, or special offers can stimulate ongoing participation. Trust and loyalty grow when community members see a tangible return on the time they invest in your brand. It's a simple yet often underestimated strategy for retaining interest and commitment.

Transparency within a brand community is non-negotiable. Be open about your successes, and more importantly, your failures. Use hardships as an opportunity to display resilience and a commitment to improvement. Members of a community appreciate honesty, which in turn fortifies the foundation of trust.

To safeguard the integrity of your brand community, set forth rules and standards of conduct. It is essential for creating a safe and welcoming environment. Without clear guidelines, communities can quickly become chaotic and uninviting. Make sure these guidelines are clearly communicated and enforced with compassion and fairness.

A successful brand community is not homogenous; it celebrates diversity and inclusivity. Encourage varying viewpoints and be open to change. Communities evolve, and a wise brand understands the need to adapt to the growing and shifting landscapes of their audiences' interests and behaviors.

To keep a finger on the community's pulse, routinely employ surveys, polls, and feedback requests. This information is priceless, offering direct insight into how your community perceives your brand, products, or services, and where there is room for enhancement. Utilize this data to make informed decisions that align with your community's desires and needs.

Lastly, measure your community's vitality through both qualitative and quantitative metrics. Engagement rates, content shares, community growth, and sentiment analysis provide a well-rounded view of the health of your brand community. Keep a close eye on these metrics to navigate and fine-tune your strategy for continuous growth and engagement.

In conclusion, building a brand community is a delicate, yet invigorating endeavor that can significantly amplify a brand's reach and resonance. It is an ongoing process of cultivating connections, initiating engaging dialogue, and providing exceptional experiences. When executed with sincerity and strategic foresight, a brand community transforms customers into loyal advocates and, ultimately, the most persuasive and credible ambassadors for your brand.

Chapter 11:
Overcoming Digital Distractions and Ad Fatigue

In the relentless tide of online noise, your message must not only resonate but also provide a beacon of relevance that guides consumers through digital distractions and ad fatigue. In this chapter, we'll explore how to create campaigns that slice through the cacophony with surgical precision, making use of strategic retargeting methods that bear in mind the delicate balance between persuasion and intrusion. As we delve into revitalizing interest in markets bombarded with advertising, you'll learn to wield innovation and creativity as your most potent weapons. Each campaign will become a crafted narrative, a distinct voice that breaks free from the echo chamber, ensuring your message is not just heard, but felt and remembered. As we empower you to captivate your audience, let's transform the challenges of the digital landscape into compelling opportunities for connection, leveraging the very distractions that once hindered us into stepping stones for engagement and brand loyalty.

Creating Campaigns That Cut Through the Noise

In an age where our senses are bombarded by digital content from every angle, creating campaigns that resonate and captivate the audience is not just advantageous; it's imperative. To truly stand out, your campaigns must slice through a thick fog of digital distractions and ad fatigue with unrivaled sharpness and clarity. How, you might ask, can such a feat be accomplished?

Success begins with getting to the heart of human emotion and using it as a compass. Tapping into the visceral responses of your audience allows you to weave a narrative that is not only appealing but also memorable. You're not selling a product; you're offering a gateway to a desired state of being. Whether that's a sense of belonging, recognition, security, or exhilaration, your campaign must transcend the digital medium and evoke these core emotions.

The distinctiveness of your message also plays a crucial role. Consider the attributes that make your brand unique. Is it your commitment to sustainability, your revolutionary approach to customer service, or perhaps your innovative product features? Whatever it is, your campaign should highlight these elements in an engaging and impactful manner. With each campaign, you're not just aiming to inform; you're striving to enlighten.

To create campaigns with stopping power, research is your ally. Analyze which content types perform best with your target demographic. Do they gravitate towards immersive video content? Or perhaps they prefer quick, digestible infographics? Once you've homed in on the medium of choice, you can tailor your campaigns to match your audience's consumption habits.

An essential factor in cutting through noise is consistency. Building campaigns on the foundational pillars of your brand's ethos and identity ensures that each message reinforces and amplifies the preceding ones. This strategy forges a stronger and more coherent brand narrative that your audience can recognize and follow amidst a sea of competing messages.

Interactivity offers a pathway for engagement that is hard for audiences to ignore. Instead of passive consumption, invite your audience to partake in the conversation. Polls, quizzes, and interactive videos are just a few avenues that can transform a one-directional pitch into a dialogue. This engagement is key to maintaining attention and fostering a deeper connection with your brand.

Timing is also of the essence. Your campaigns should seize the moment, responding to current events, trends, or seasonal shifts with agility. This not only keeps your brand topical but also telegraphs a sense of immediacy that prompts action. However, exercise caution; align your campaigns with events and trends that resonate with your brand values to maintain authenticity.

Personalization is not just a buzzword; it is a ticket to individual hearts and minds. When you tailor content to meet specific audience segments' preferences and behaviors, you signal that you understand and value their unique needs. Use data analytics to inform personalization strategies, thereby ensuring that your campaign messages strike a deeply personal chord.

Don't underestimate the power of storytelling. A compelling story can charge through the rabble like a bolt of lightning. Engage your audience with stories that showcase real-life applications of your product or service, complete with characters they can relate to and outcomes they aspire to achieve. Be sure that the story aligns seamlessly with your brand narrative to ensure authenticity.

Incorporate social proof to bolster credibility. Testimonials, reviews, and user-generated content act as a force multiplier. They provide tangible proof that others have embarked on the journey you're advocating for and have emerged satisfied. People tend to follow the lead of others they admire or relate to, making social proof an invaluable asset in your campaign arsenal.

Exclusivity has its allure. Crafting campaigns that offer exclusive insights, deals, or access can create a sense of urgency and privilege.

This approach plays into the principle of scarcity which, when used ethically, can be a powerful motivator for audiences to act quickly lest they miss out on a coveted opportunity.

A multi-channel approach ensures that your campaign reaches audiences wherever they are. However, don't spread yourself thin by trying to be everywhere at once. Choose channels wisely based on where your target audience spends the most time and tailors your messaging to fit the norms and expectations of each platform.

Remember that visual aesthetics cannot be downplayed. A visually striking campaign can capture attention instantaneously. Invest in high-quality graphics, vibrant color schemes, and professional photography that embody your brand's tone and message.

Lastly, resilience is critical. Not every campaign will be a home run, and the digital landscape is ever-evolving. Be prepared to monitor, adapt, and iterate on your campaigns based on performance data and feedback. This agility allows you to refine and optimize your messaging, ensuring your campaigns remain sharp and effective over time.

By leveraging the potent combination of emotional resonance, authenticity, interactivity, and personalized storytelling, your campaigns stand a compelling chance of cutting through digital noise. This is not just about capturing fleeting attention; it's about forging lasting connections that drive engagement and action. With each campaign you launch, you're not just filling space in the digital ecosystem—you're illuminating it with your unique brand story that refuses to be ignored.

Employing Retargeting Without Being Intrusive

In a world awash with digital content, the art of retargeting stands as a beacon for businesses vying to capture their audience's fleeting attention without falling into the abyss of intrusiveness. Retargeting, when done with finesse, can be a subtle nudge rather than a jarring push, keeping brands gently present in the minds of their prospects.

Retargeting operates on a simple premise: remind visitors of your product or service after they leave your website without completing a purchase. However, the line between reminding and intruding is fine, and crossing it can lead to ad fatigue and resentment. The following strategies will help you strike that balance and leverage retargeting as an effective, non-invasive tool in your digital repertoire.

Firstly, timing is everything. Initiating a retargeting campaign immediately after a visitor leaves your site can feel aggressive. Allow a grace period before your ads begin to appear on their screens. A delayed approach demonstrates respect for the consumer's online experience and decision-making process.

Next, frequency capping is your ally. There is a temptation to bombard your audience with repetitive ads to engrain your brand in their minds. Resist this urge. Set a limit to the number of times your ad will appear to the same person in a given timeframe. This strategy is less about scarcity and more about preserving the aura of your brand without overwhelming potential customers.

Customization is the key. Retargeting gives you a golden opportunity to present personalized content tailored to the user's previous interactions. Use data intelligently to curate ads that reflect the unique interests and behaviors of your audience. By customizing your approach, you create a meaningful connection rather than a generic call-to-action.

Don't underestimate the power of segmentation. Customize the retargeting experience to different user groups based on their position in the sales funnel. A new visitor who viewed a product might respond differently to an ad compared to someone who abandoned a shopping cart. Segmenting your audience enables more precise messaging that resonates with where they are in the buyer's journey.

Consider the content of your retargeted ads. Rather than just pushing for a sale, offer value. Educational content, special discounts, and helpful reminders about items left in a shopping cart can serve as the gentle reminder that nudges users back to your site without irritation.

Encourage the opt-out option. This might seem counterintuitive, but making it easy for users to opt out of retargeting ads can benefit your brand's perception. It demonstrates a transparent and consumer-first approach, showing that you respect their online space and choices.

Mix up your creative elements. Repeatedly seeing the same ad can lead to annoyance and desensitization. Instead, develop a variety of creative assets for your campaign. Alternating visuals and messaging can maintain interest and prevent your brand from becoming stale or irritating.

Engage in cross-channel retargeting. Don't limit your retargeting efforts to a single platform. By carefully placing retargeting ads across different channels, you can create a cohesive brand narrative that gently accompanies your audience throughout their digital journey, instead of bombarding them on a single platform.

Monitor and adapt based on feedback. Pay attention to how audiences interact with your retargeting ads. If you notice a decline in engagement or an increase in negative feedback, it's time to revise your tactics. Adapting to your audience's response is crucial to maintain a positive brand image.

Exercise ethical remarketing. Just because technology allows you to track user behavior extensively doesn't mean you should use it to its fullest invasive potential. Be mindful of privacy concerns and focus on creating a retargeting experience that is both ethical and effective.

Retarget with a storytelling approach. Narratives can guide your retargeting efforts by creating a continuation of the story that began with the user's first interaction. This could evolve through a sequence of ads that unfold over time, building curiosity and engagement without direct pressure to make an immediate purchase.

Remember to test and optimize. Like all marketing efforts, retargeting requires testing different strategies to see what works best. A/B testing can be particularly useful in fine-tuning your approach, ensuring that your retargeting initiatives hit the mark without becoming a source of irritation.

Lastly, always prioritize the user experience. Retargeting should enhance the online journey, not detract from it. By understanding your audience and providing them with relevant, engaging content at a respectful frequency, you elevate your brand in a crowded digital landscape without becoming intrusive.

Successful retargeting in the digital age is a balancing act. It demands an ongoing commitment to understanding your audience, as well as an agility to refine tactics that protect the integrity of the user experience. Done correctly, retargeting can be a potent, non-intrusive way to remain top of mind and gently guide your audience back to your offerings.

Renewing Interest in Saturated Markets

In an era where digital markets are becoming increasingly saturated, marketers confront the challenge of capturing and sustaining audience interest. A deep understanding of the market dynamics and consumer psyche is your most potent advantage. Distinguishing yourself in a saturated market requires inventive tactics and a commitment to understanding what truly resonates with your audience.

Digital saturation can lead to consumer indifference where advertisements become part of the noise. Therefore, it starts with assessing what's out there. Scrutinize the prevailing strategies and the needs they meet—or neglect. In doing this research, you can form the foundation of a plan that doesn't just add to the noise, but intelligently disrupts it.

To renew interest in a saturated market, you must focus on segmentation. Understand that within the wide expanse of your market, there are niches longing for attention. Tailoring your messaging to these specific segments presents your brand as a specialized solution rather than a one-size-fits-all echo.

Consider leveraging exclusivity to spark renewed interest. Craft compelling narratives that position your products or services as limited commodities. This notion of scarcity can rekindle a sense of urgency and draw your audience back in. By presenting an opportunity that appears fleeting, you may invigorate market segments that have grown indifferent to the abundance of choices.

Amidst the backdrop of countless companies clawing for attention, establishing a unique brand personality is indispensable. Ask yourself, what can we offer that transcends our product or service? This often involves cultivating a brand mythology, imbuing your company with stories and qualities that are memorable and shareable.

Interactive marketing initiatives can also serve to draw in an audience that has grown weary of traditional advertisements. Hosting virtual events, polls, or contests that invite participation signals that you value your customers' input and engagement. This active inclusion stands out in a static landscape of passive marketing tactics.

Refresh your content regularly. In a world where trend lifecycles are shrinking by the minute, being seen as a trendsetter rather than a follower can make all the difference. Monitor social cues and harness insights to maintain relevancy. Your content strategy should be nimble, adaptive, and always one step ahead.

Investing in new platforms can also break through saturation. While there is a converging focus on certain social media giants, exploring emerging platforms can help you tap untouched user bases. Early adaptation comes with risks, but it also places you in a pioneering stance that could pay dividends.

Recognize and embrace the power of micro-influencers. Their niche followings are often highly engaged and loyal, presenting an opportunity for specific market penetration. Collaborations with these influencers can add a genuine voice to your brand and transfer trust to your products or services.

Moreover, reexamine your value proposition. With consumers bombarded by similar messages, redefine what sets you apart. It's not about overhauling what you offer, but rather highlighting aspects not previously considered or underrepresented in your messaging. This reframing can transform perspectives and re-interest consumers in your market.

Customer feedback loops are key to staying dynamic in saturated markets. Actively seek out and listen to customer feedback. This loop not only signals to your customers that you value their experience, but it also provides vital information for iterative improvements and innovation.

Another approach is to rethink personalization. Beyond just using a customer's name, it's about crafting a user experience that feels unique to each person. Analysis of user behavior and preferences allows for a predictive model that recommends relevant content, creating a resonant and tailored consumer journey.

In saturated markets where novelty has depreciated, the rediscovery of authenticity has a magnetic pull. This means stripping back the overly-manufactured sheen that many digital campaigns have and returning to the roots of your brand's ethos. A genuine story, untold aspects of your founding, or employee spotlights add a layer of authenticity that cuts through the market's saturation.

Lastly, bear in mind that value-driven marketing can become your greatest differentiator. Consumers in a saturated market are looking for brands that stand for something. Embedding your values into your campaigns, showing not just what you sell but why you sell it, and the impact of your work can galvanize a community around your brand.

To sum up, the crux of renewing interest in saturated markets lies in thinking outside the conventions. It's about reconceptualizing rather than conforming, about genuine connections over broad appeal, and about fine-tuning your strategies to the ever-changing heartbeat of consumer interests. In this digital age, where everything seems to have been done, it's the innovators and authentic storytellers who will capture and keep the market's attention.

Chapter 12:
Ethical Persuasion in Digital Marketing

As we pivot from overcoming the hurdles of ad fatigue and digital distractions, Chapter 12 delves into the cornerstone of long-lasting success in digital marketing: ethics. Ethical persuasion isn't just about staying compliant with regulations like GDPR; it's the lifeblood of building trust and enduring relationships with your audience. The digital realm is rife with opportunities to sway minds and convert clicks into customers, yet it rests upon the marketers' shoulders to balance potent persuasion with upright honesty and unyielding transparency. This chapter is a deep dive into the quintessence of ethical marketing practices, illustrating how integrity is intricately linked to the undying loyalty of your consumers. Here, we unmask the strategies behind ethical persuasion—ones that reassure your audience of their valued privacy, ones that cement your place as a trustworthy authority without compromising on ambition—and how these practices aren't simply nice-to-haves but rather necessities for sustainable brand growth in the digital expanse.

Consent and Privacy in the Age of GDPR

In crafting your digital persuasion blueprint, let us not overlook the significance of consent and privacy—terms that have been rewritten in the playbook of digital marketing since the inception of the General Data Protection Regulation (GDPR). Comprehending and abiding by GDPR is not only mandatory for compliance but is also pivotal in fostering trust with your audience, ultimately empowering your digital marketing strategies.

GDPR, as daunting as it may sound, is essentially Europe's framework for data protection laws. It has global implications and enforces stringent rules on how businesses must handle the personal data of individuals residing in the European Union. But why should this matter in your grand scheme of digital marketing? Because in an interconnected digital ecosystem, geographic boundaries blur, and a click on your content could be from anywhere in the world.

To align with GDPR, obtaining clear consent is fundamental. Consent under GDPR is not a mere tick box exercise; it is an affirmative action. In this context, marketers must ensure that they seek explicit permission before gathering any data from their audience. This means being transparent about what data you collect and how you intend to use it and giving individuals the power to easily withdraw their consent should they choose to do so.

However, consent is just the tip of the iceberg. Privacy by design, another key aspect of GDPR, requires you to incorporate data protection into your digital initiatives from the outset. This involves assessing and mitigating privacy risks during development stages, not as an afterthought, to ensure that user data is secure throughout all processes.

Your digital marketing techniques must be adjusted to accommodate these requirements while still achieving your goals. Building complex data profiles of users, a previously common practice, demands thorough justification and transparency. Instead, enriched audience segmentation that respects user privacy is essential, which requires a shift in perspective yet opens a door to create more meaningful customer relationships.

Moreover, GDPR strengthens the rights of individuals in the digital age. One such right is the 'Right to be Forgotten,' which essentially allows individuals to have their data erased. This affects how marketers maintain contact databases and utilize retargeting strategies. Practices must now include easy-to-use mechanisms allowing individuals to erase their digital footprint from your databases.

Adapting to these changes, let's craft experiences that prioritize respect for personal boundaries. This means less intrusive tracking, more engaging and valuable content strategies that compel voluntary data sharing, and a preference for quality interactions over quantity in data collection.

Remember, trust is the cornerstone of any successful marketing endeavor. By adhering to GDPR, you're emphatically stating, "Your privacy matters." This boosts consumer confidence in your brand, a priceless currency in today's market where skepticism towards data misuse is at an all-time high.

Audit your current practices and scrutinize each step of your data collection processes. Determine whether each piece of user information is essential or if you're stockpiling data without clear purpose. Shift your mindset from collecting as much data as possible to collecting the right data with purpose and consent.

Imagine the long-term value you create by respecting and upholding user privacy. This isn't just a regulatory hoop to jump through; it's an opportunity to showcase your brand's integrity and dedication to user empowerment and trust-building. GDPR, in essence, has compelled the marketing world to elevate its standards—a movement that can only improve the industry as a whole.

With GDPR as a jumping-off point, widen your perspective to grasp global privacy concerns and anticipate upcoming regulations, such as the California Consumer Privacy Act (CCPA) and others around the world. Tailor your marketing operations not only to meet existing legal requirements but to exceed them, positioning your brand as the gold standard in user data respect and protection.

Utilize technology to streamline GDPR compliance. Invest in CRM systems, email marketing platforms, and analytics tools that keep consent and privacy at the forefront. These technologies can help automate consent records, manage user preferences, and ensure that your marketing activities stay on the right side of the law.

Let's view GDPR as a catalyst for innovation and an invitation to delve into a marketing approach that champions transparency and prioritizes the consumer's choice and control over their data. Craft marketing campaigns that inspire action, foster loyalty, and nurture an environment where consent is given freely and with enthusiasm.

In closing, embed the ethos of GDPR into the DNA of your digital persuasion strategy. Create a narrative that resonates with your audience's increased awareness of their digital rights. Your marketing campaigns should not only speak to your audience's needs and desires but also reassure them that their personal data is held in high regard, escorted by diligent stewardship and unwavering ethics. That's a brand worth talking about, worth engaging with, and, undoubtedly, worth trusting in the digital age of persuasion.

Balancing Persuasion with Honesty and Transparency

In the realm of digital marketing, persuasion is a cornerstone for driving engagement and conversion. Yet, it's vital to remember that effective persuasion must be grounded in honesty and transparency. The online world offers myriad avenues to reach audiences, but your success hinges on the trust you build with them.

Honesty is more than a moral compass in digital marketing; it's a strategic asset. Consumers are savvy and can detect insincerity in a heartbeat. When your messaging rings true, you're not just abiding by ethical principles; you're also cultivating an authentic connection with your audience. This relationship bears the fruits of loyalty and a strong brand reputation.

Transparency isn't just about revealing the fine print or complying with regulations. It's about letting your audience see through the veils of marketing speak, understanding your ethos, your processes, and your values. When your audience feels like insiders, they're more likely to become advocates for your brand.

Effectual persuasion doesn't manipulate; it informs. It invites the audience to make decisions based on a clear understanding of the benefits and any potential drawbacks. This approach can be transformative, turning passive observers into active participants in the story of your brand.

But how does one strike a balance between persuasive digital marketing and maintaining integrity? It starts with a commitment to presenting your products or services in a light that's both flattering and factual. It means avoiding the pitfalls of overpromising and underdelivering at all costs.

Storytelling is a powerful tool in the digital marketer's repertoire. Your narrative should resonate with truth, painting a picture of your offerings that aligns with the user experience. Exaggerations and falsehoods may snag a quick sale but will ultimately unravel the fabric of trust you've woven with your base.

Audit your marketing materials with a critical eye. Is every claim you make supportable? Do your testimonials reflect actual customer feedback? When citing statistics or achievements, ensure they are accurate and current. Erring on the side of caution in these areas shields your brand from potential backlash.

Transparency extends to your digital footprint and how you handle data. In a world where privacy concerns are escalating, your transparency policy can be a beacon that shines brighter than your competition's. Handle data ethically, communicate your policies clearly, and follow through on your promises.

Incorporate transparency in your pricing as well. Hidden fees or unexpected costs are a surefire way to erode trust. When your audience understands exactly what they're paying for and why they feel respected and in control—a critical element in a successful persuasive strategy.

Consumer feedback is a gold mine for any digital marketer. Act on it, showcase changes that have been made in response to feedback, and you'll send a powerful message that you're listening and evolving. This loop of feedback and improvement demonstrates a commitment to excellence that persuasively enhances your brand's appeal.

Empathy should be woven into your persuasive strategies. Understand and acknowledge the challenges and pains your audience may face. By aligning your marketing efforts with the needs and concerns of your audience, your brand becomes more than a seller—it becomes a partner in their journey.

The core of balancing persuasion with honesty and transparency resides in maintaining a customer-centric approach. Put yourself in the shoes of your customers: What information would you want? What truths would compel you to remain loyal to a brand? Answer these questions openly in your marketing efforts, and you'll find that ethical persuasion nurtures long-term, profitable relationships.

Finally, don't shy away from discussing the limitations of what you offer. Every product or service has its limits, and by openly discussing them, you're affirming to your audience that you value their experience above the sale. This forthrightness is refreshing and builds a foundation of trust that can weather any storm.

In conclusion, balancing persuasion with honesty and transparency isn't merely an ethical choice; it's a strategic imperative. Today's consumers crave authenticity and reward those who deliver it with brand loyalty and advocacy. As you weave this balance throughout your digital marketing campaigns, what you're truly building is a lasting legacy for your brand that will resonate for years to come.

The Long-Term Value of Ethical Marketing Practices

Within the realm of digital marketing, ethical practices aren't just an idealistic approach; they're a foundational element that can significantly impact the longevity and success of your brand. The long-term value of ethical marketing practices stands as a testament to the power of trust and credibility in an increasingly skeptical online world.

Trust is the cornerstone of any successful relationship, and this is no different when it comes to the bond between a brand and its customers. Ethical marketing practices nurture this trust, transforming one-time buyers into loyal enthusiasts. When customers believe in the sincerity behind your message, they're more likely to engage with your content and champion your brand.

Implementing ethical marketing strategies can also enhance brand reputation. Reputation isn't built overnight, but is cultivated through consistently demonstrating integrity and genuine value. It makes a resounding statement to potential customers who are witnessing your brand's interactions and assessing your worthiness.

Consider the impact of ethical marketing on customer satisfaction. When customers are treated with respect and not misled by exaggerated claims or deceptive tactics, their overall satisfaction with your brand increases. This satisfaction is a potent indicator that feeds into positive online reviews, referrals, and testimonials—key drivers of organic growth.

Certainly, ethical marketing practices play a significant role in risk mitigation. In the digital age, where a single misstep can spread like wildfire across social media and news outlets, maintaining an ethical stance shields your brand from public relations nightmares and costly legal challenges.

The notion of brand differentiation is also vital. As markets become more saturated, the ability to stand out becomes increasingly difficult. Commitment to ethical practices sets you apart and can attract customers who are disillusioned with the status quo. In essence, your integrity becomes your brand's unique selling proposition.

Another aspect to recognize is the long-term financial benefits. Although implementing ethical practices may not always deliver immediate financial gains, it's an investment in sustainable growth. Customers with favorable perceptions of a brand's ethics are more likely to pay a premium for its products or services, translating into a stronger bottom line over time.

Employee morale and retention can flourish under ethical marketing standards. Teams that work for ethically responsible companies often exhibit higher levels of commitment, productivity, and job satisfaction. This internal culture reflects externally, too, as customers often sense and align with the positive energy of happy and engaged employees.

Moreover, consider the role of ethical marketing in innovation. When you're committed to honesty and transparency, you're compelled to improve your offerings and find novel solutions that genuinely add value to your customers' lives. This dedication to authentic improvement drives innovation and keeps your brand ahead of the curve.

Let's not forget the legal aspect. Adhering to ethical norms ensures compliance with the law, which is increasingly focusing on protecting consumer rights in the digital domain. By proactively adopting ethical advertising methods, you safeguard your company from substantial legal fines and the associated damage to your reputation.

Investing in the future isn't just about technology and trends. It's also about investing in ethical foundations that will underpin your marketing efforts. As privacy concerns spike and regulations tighten, being ahead in ethical marketing will ensure you're not scrambling to catch up, but rather, leading the charge.

Customer empowerment also has a hand in play. Empowered customers with access to information like never before will respect brands that don't exploit their data but instead, use it to build better experiences. This empowerment leads to stronger customer-brand connections that can weather market fluctuations and shifts in consumer behavior.

Companies focused on ethical marketing practices are often viewed as thought leaders in their respective industries. They set the benchmark for others to follow, wielding the influence not through manipulation, but through integrity and principled action. This positions them as industry leaders that others look up to and aspire to emulate.

There's a profound social impact to consider as well. Brands practicing ethical marketing contribute to the larger social good by prioritizing messages that are inclusive, respectful, and community-oriented. As consumers grow increasingly conscious of social issues, they gravitate towards brands that align with their values.

Lastly, embracing ethical marketing is about building a legacy. Brands that last are those that have built a reputation for being trustworthy and reliable. In the digital marketing landscape, your brand's legacy will be shaped by the consistent ethical stance you maintain—defining not only your present success but also charting the course of your future.

The value of ethical marketing practices extends far beyond the immediate, transcending transactions to sow the seeds of trust, reputation, innovation, and leadership. Ethical marketing is not simply a good practice—it's a strategic imperative for any brand aspiring to thrive in the complex ecosystem of digital marketing.

Chapter 13:
The Future of Digital Persuasion

As we look to the horizon of digital marketing, it's evident that the art of persuasion will continue to evolve in tandem with technological advancements and shifting consumer behaviors. The key to harnessing the true potential of digital persuasion lies not only in adapting to the changes but in anticipating them, staying a step ahead of the curve, and understanding the underlying currents shaping the digital landscape.

Imagine a marketing world where personalization is not just a strategy but a baseline expectation. Data-driven insights and AI algorithms will become even more sophisticated, crafting customer journeys so individually tailored that each interaction feels personal, unique, and incredibly persuasive. This depth of personalization will foster stronger connections between brands and consumers, allowing for an unprecedented level of engagement and brand loyalty.

A video isn't just another content type; it's set to be the cornerstone of digital persuasion. With the rise of virtual reality (VR) and augmented reality (AR), immersive experiences will become the norm, crafting narratives that allow consumers to experience products and services in compelling, emotionally impactful ways. This isn't just video marketing; it's creating a world where your audience can step inside the story.

The proliferation of social media platforms has democratized influence, and this trend will continue to shape the mechanisms of digital persuasion. The key will be in the strategic convergence of authenticity and influence, where influencers and brands collaborate to create genuine connections and relatable content that resonates with audiences on a profound level.

Search engine optimization (SEO) and search engine marketing (SEM) may soon be revolutionized by AI that can interpret not just data but meaning, intent, and contextual relevance with a finesse that mimics human understanding. This will transform how we think about being "found" online, making search results more intuitive, and organically matching consumers with content that feels like it was crafted just for them.

Analytics will go beyond mere numbers to tell the story behind those numbers, enabling marketers to peer into the psyche of their audience with clarity and depth. A/B testing will be refined into a process that doesn't just compare outcomes but understands why one option prevails, giving marketers forensic insight into the art of persuasion.

When it comes to content, the future lies in dynamic, interactive formats that do more than inform, they engage. We're entering an era where the audience becomes part of the narrative, contributing to and altering the story as it unfolds. This interactive push will not only captivate audiences but will keep them invested, turning passive consumers into active brand advocates.

Influencer marketing will mature into a realm of co-created experiences and values-driven partnerships. Brands and influencers alike will have to navigate this landscape with a keen sense of ethics and responsibility, making sure that the persuasive power they wield is done so with honesty and transparency.

Engagement and community building will continue to be the bedrock of digital marketing, but the strategies employed will become more advanced. Brands will evolve into cultural hubs, offering a sense of belonging and a shared purpose that extends well beyond the products or services they sell. Communities will not just be markets; they'll be movements.

The battle against ad fatigue and digital distractions will rage on, challenging marketers to create campaigns that can cut through an ever-thickening fog of content. Success will hinge on innovation, agility, and a willingness to take risks, forging new paths to capture attention and sustain interest in markets flooded with stimuli.

As we move forward, ethical persuasion will become more than an obligation—it will be a competitive advantage. In a world where privacy concerns and consent are paramount, brands that can skillfully navigate these waters while maintaining trust will outshine their less scrupulous counterparts, building enduring bonds with consumers.

From AI and VR to deep analytics and ethical considerations, the future of digital persuasion is vibrant and varied. It's a landscape that will require continuous learning, adaptation, and a deep understanding of not just where the digital world is now, but where it's heading.

Marketers must become architects of experiences, innovators of engagement, and stewards of trust. They must craft not just campaigns, but journeys; not just narratives, but experiences; not just connections, but relationships. Digital persuasion is set to become less about the pitch and more about the dialogue, less about the sale and more about the connection.

Standing at the threshold of this future, we have an opportunity to redefine marketing in profound ways. As you close this book and embark on your own journey of digital persuasion, remember that the most effective strategies will be those that are fluid, responsive, and above all, human. The future is not just digital; it's personal, ethical, and full of potential. It's a canvas that's vast and ever-changing, and it's yours to paint.

By embracing these future trends and tools with a spirit of innovation and a commitment to genuine connection, the possibilities for digital persuasion are limitless. The future is calling—how will you answer?

Appendix A:
Digital Marketing Resource Toolkit

Welcome to your Digital Marketing Resource Toolkit, a carefully curated collection designed to support your endeavors in the world of digital persuasion. This is more than just a list; it's an armory of tools that, when wielded with skill and strategic insight, will forge the path to your success in the digital landscape.

Your Toolkit Components

Keyword Research Tools: Unearth the words and phrases that resonate with your audience and ensure your content is discovered online.

SEO Analytics Platforms: Refine your content with surgical precision, making certain that your messaging is both visible and impactful.

Content Creation Software: From breathtaking visuals to captivating written narratives, empower your storytelling with these tools.

Email Automation Systems: Engage your community with personalized, timely, and relevant conversations that convert.

Social Media Management Suites: Orchestrate your brand's social symphony, fostering relationships and building your digital tribe.

Video Editing Applications: Sculpt your video content into persuasive masterpieces, carving out emotional connections with your viewers.

Conversion Rate Optimization Tools: Master the art of the tweak, transforming passive viewers into active participants and customers.

Customer Relationship Management (CRM) Platforms: Build and nurture relationships at scale, converting leads into loyal brand advocates.

Webinar and Live Streaming Software: Break down the barriers with live interactions that captivate, educate, and engage.

Advertising Platforms: Leverage these powerhouses to place your persuasive messages directly into the line of sight of your ideal audience.

Influencer Marketing Databases: Connect with voices that resonate and amplify your message through authentic partnerships.

Graphic Design Tools: Visual aesthetics are crucial; these tools will ensure your brand shines in its best light.

As you navigate through the ebbs and flows of digital marketing, remember that the key to success is in how effectively you can use these tools to convey your message. It isn't about the volume of tools in your toolkit, but the mastery of their usage. Be patient; domination in the digital world is a craft refined over time.

Tailoring Your Toolkit to Your Needs

No two digital landscapes are identical, and your toolkit should be as unique as your digital footprint. Assess the impact of each tool by leaning on analytics and user feedback. A/B testing these tools and strategies is not just recommended—it is essential for honing your skills and sharpening your strategy.

Remember that personalization is the ultimate persuasion tool. Let your toolkit reflect your brand's unique voice and values. Align your tools with your persuasion strategy to ensure consistency across all digital touchpoints.

Evolution of Your Toolkit

The only constant in digital marketing is change. Embrace this perpetual evolution. Update your toolkit with emerging technologies, and stay agile in your approach. The future of digital persuasion isn't written—it's created by marketers who dare to innovate and inspire.

Above all, wield these tools with integrity, and let your passion for your vision guide the way. May your strategic use of these resources bring you closer to your goals, with each click, each campaign, and each connection. Here's to your continued growth and to the remarkable journey ahead.

Appendix B:
Persuasion Checklist for Digital Marketers

As you've traversed the landscape of digital marketing through the pages of this book, you have been equipped with a myriad of strategies designed to harness the power of persuasion. Approaching the digital sphere, your arsenal should be laden with tactics that are not only effective but also resonate with your audience on a personal level. Let's ensure that before launching your next campaign, you've got everything in place to captivate, engage, and convert. This checklist will serve as your compass, guiding you through the critical elements of digital persuasion so that you can create campaigns that leave a lasting impression and drive results.

The Persuasion Essentials

Understand Your Audience: Have you deeply researched your target demographics' pain points, desires, and digital habits?

Principles of Influence: Have you incorporated the six principles by Cialdini (reciprocity, commitment & consistency, social proof, authority, liking, scarcity) into your strategy?

Value Proposition: Is your value proposition crystal clear and articulated in a way that shows undeniable benefit to your audience?

Content that Converts: Does your content not just inform but also inspire action? Is it optimized for each stage of the user's journey?

Visual Persuasion: Are your visual elements (photos, videos, infographics) crafted to evoke emotions and tell a compelling story?

Multi-Channel Integration: Have you created a seamless narrative across all platforms where your audience can interact with your brand?

Social Proof: Did you use reviews, testimonials, case studies, and user-generated content to build trust and credibility?

Call to Action: Are your CTAs persuasive and clearly guiding the user to the next step?

SEO and SEM: Have you utilized SEO and SEM to ensure that your message is not just persuasive but also discoverable?

Data-Driven Decisions: Are all your efforts backed by data to eliminate guesswork and measure the true impact of your persuasion tactics?

Advanced Persuasion Techniques

Emotional Triggers: Have you targeted the emotional triggers that can lead to higher engagement and conversion rates?

Storytelling: Does your campaign narrative leverage the power of storytelling to create a memorable and relatable brand experience?

Exclusivity: Have you created a sense of exclusivity or urgency that encourages immediate action?

Personalization: Are you personalizing experiences at scale, acknowledging your audience as individuals with unique needs and preferences?

Technology Utilization: Have you leveraged AI, chatbots, or other emerging technologies to personalize and streamline the persuasion process?

Testing and Optimization: Is your strategy built on the foundation of continuous A/B testing and optimization for improved outcomes?

Maintaining Ethical Standards

Honesty: Is your marketing messaging honest and clear, free from misleading information and false promises?

Transparency: Have you maintained transparency regarding product information, endorsements, and data usage?

Respect for Privacy: Does your strategy respect user privacy and comply with regulations like the GDPR?

In an age where attention is the currency of the digital realm, mastering the art of persuasion is not just about having a message—it's about making that message matter to those who hear it. Use this checklist as an iterative tool, revisiting it with each campaign to refine and enhance your approach. Your capacity to influence and inspire is limitless when grounded in strategy, creativity, and an unwavering commitment to your audience. Consider each point on this checklist not as a box to be checked but as a stepping stone towards building a more persuasive, powerful, and profitable digital presence. Let your campaigns be the benchmark of innovation and integrity, capturing hearts and minds in a world that is constantly evolving.